PREFACE

THAT the subject on which this humble volume treats is vastly
solemn, and deeply searching, every true believer in Jesus
must acknowledge. The existing necessity for such a work
has long impressed itself upon the Author's mind. While
other and abler writers are employing their pens, either in
defending the outposts of Christianity, or in arousing a slumbering church to an increased intensity of personal and combined action in the great work of Christian benevolence, he
has felt that if he might but be instrumental, in ever so humble
a way, of occasionally withdrawing the eye of the believer
from the dazzling and almost bewildering movements around
him, and fixing it upon the state of HIS OWN PERSONAL RE-
LIGION, he would be rendering the Christian church a service,
not the less needed and important in her present elevated and
excited position.

It must be admitted, that the character and the tendencies
of the age are not favourable to deep and mature reflection
upon the hidden, spiritual life of the soul. Whirled along as
the church of God is, in her brilliant path of benevolent enterprise,—deeply engaged in concerting and in carrying out new
and far-reaching plans of aggression upon the dominion of
sin,—and compelled in one hand to hold the spiritual sword in
defence of the faith which, with the other, she is up-building,
—but few energies are left, and but little time is afforded, for
close, faithful, and frequent dealing with the personal and
spiritual state of grace in the soul; which, in consequence of
thus being overlooked and uncultivated, may fall into a state

of the deepest and most painful declension. "They made me keeper of the vineyards, but *mine own* vineyard have I not kept." (Sol. Song i. 6).

It is, then, the humble design of the writer in the present work, for a while to withdraw the mind from the consideration of the mere externals of Christianity, and to aid the believer in answering the solemn and searching inquiry,— "What is the present spiritual state of my soul before God?" In the following pages he is exhorted to forget the Christian profession he sustains, the party badge he wears, and the distinctive name by which he is known among men,—to turn aside for a brief hour from all religious duties, engagements, and excitement, and to look this question fully and fairly in the face.

With human wisdom and eloquence the Author has not seen fit to load and adorn his work: the subject presented itself to his mind in too solemn and awful an aspect for this. The ground he traversed he felt to be so holy, that he had need to put off the shoes from his feet, and to lay aside everything that was not in strict harmony with the spiritual character of his theme. That the traces of human imperfection may be found on every page, no one can be more conscious than the Author,—no one more deeply humbled. Indeed, so affecting to his own mind has been the conviction of the feeble manner in which the subject is treated, that but for a deep sense of its vast importance, and the demand that exists for its discussion in almost any shape, he would more than once have withdrawn his book from the press. May the Spirit of God accompany its perusal with power and unction, and to Him, as unto the Father and the Son, shall be ascribed the glory!

LEAMINGTON SPA,
  Sept., 1841.

PERSONAL DECLENSION AND REVIVAL

OF

RELIGION IN THE SOUL

PERSONAL DECLENSION

AND REVIVAL OF
RELIGION IN THE SOUL

OCTAVIUS WINSLOW, D.D.

THE BANNER OF TRUTH TRUST

THE BANNER OF TRUTH TRUST
3 Murrayfield Road, Edinburgh EH12 6EL
PO Box 621, Carlisle, Pennsylvania 17013, USA

*

First published 1841
First Banner of Truth Trust edition 1960
Reprinted 1962
Reprinted as a paperback 1978
ISBN 0 85151 261 5

Printed and bound in Great Britain by
Hazell Watson & Viney Ltd
Aylesbury, Bucks

CONTENTS

CONTENTS

CHAPTER I

INCIPIENT DECLENSION

" The backslider in heart."—Prov. xiv. 14.

IF there is one consideration more humbling than another to a spiritually-minded believer, it is, that, after all God has done for him,—after all the rich displays of his grace, the patience and tenderness of his instructions, the repeated discipline of his covenant, the tokens of love received, and the lessons of experience learned, there should still exist in the heart a principle, the tendency of which is to secret, perpetual, and alarming departure from God. Truly, there is in this solemn fact, that which might well lead to the deepest self-abasement before Him.

If, in the present early stage of our inquiry into this subject, we might be permitted to assign a cause for the growing power which this latent, subtle principle is allowed to exert in the soul, we would refer to the believer's constant forgetfulness of the truth, that there is no essential element in divine grace that can secure it from the deepest declension; that, if left to its self-sustaining energy, such are the hostile influences by which it is surrounded, such the severe assaults to which it is exposed, and such the feeble resistance it is capable of exerting, there is not a moment—splendid though its former victories may have been—in which the incipient and secret progress of declension may not have commenced and be going forward in the soul! There is a proneness in us to *deify* the graces of the Spirit. We often think of faith and love, and their kindred graces, as though they were essentially omnipotent; forgetting that though they undoubtedly are divine in their origin, spiritual in their nature, and sanctifying in their effects, they yet are sustained by no self-supporting power, but by constant communications of life and nourishment from Jesus; that, the moment of their being left to their inherent strength, is the moment of their certain declension and decay.

We must here, however, guard a precious and important truth; viz., the *indestructible nature* of true grace. Divine grace in the soul can never really die; true faith can never utterly and finally fail. We are speaking now but of their *decay*. A flower may droop, and yet live: a plant may be sickly, and yet not die. In the lowest stage of spiritual declension, in the feeblest state of grace, there is a life that never dies. In the midst of all his startings aside, the ebb and the flow, the wandering and the restoring, the believer in Jesus is " kept by the power of God through faith unto salvation." He cannot utterly fall; he cannot finally be lost. The immutability of God keeps him,—the covenant of grace keeps him,—the finished work of Jesus keeps him,—the indwelling of the Spirit keeps him, and keeps him to eternal glory. We say, then, true grace is indestructible grace; it can never die. But it may *decay*; and to the consideration of this solemn and important subject, the reader's serious attention is now invited. We propose to exhibit the subject of Personal Declension of Religion in the Soul in some of its varied and prominent forms and phases, and to direct to those means which God has ordained and blessed to its restoration and revival.

Believing, as we do, that no child of God ever recedes into a state of inward declension and outward backsliding, but by slow and gradual steps; and believing, too, that a process of spiritual decay may be going forward within the secret recesses of the soul, and not a suspicion or a fear be awakened in the mind of the believer; we feel it of the deepest moment that this state should first be brought to view in its incipient and concealed form. May the Lord the Spirit fill the writer's and the reader's mind with light, the heart with lowliness, and raise and fix the eye of faith simply and solely upon Jesus, as we proceed in the unfolding of a theme so purely spiritual and so deeply heart-searching!

We commence with a brief exposition of a doctrine which must be regarded as forming the groundwork of our subject; viz., THE LIFE OF GOD IN THE SOUL OF MAN. The believer in Jesus is a partaker of the divine nature. 2 Pet. i. 4. He is " born of the Spirit "; Christ dwelleth in him by faith; and this constitutes his new and spiritual life. A single but emphatic expression of the apostle's, unfolds the doctrine and confirms the fact, " Christ in you." Col. i. 27. It is not so much that the *believer lives*, as that *Christ lives in him*. Thus the apostle expresses it: " I am crucified with Christ: nevertheless I live; yet not I, but Christ liveth in me." Do we look at the history of Paul as illustrative of the doctrine? Behold the grand secret of his extraordinary life. He lived unreservedly *for* Christ; and the spring of it was, Christ lived spiritually *in* him. This it was that rendered him so profound in wisdom, rich in knowledge, bold in preaching, undaunted in zeal, unwearied in toil, patient in suffering, and successful in labour;— Christ lived in him. And this forms the high and holy life of every child of God;—" Christ who is *our* life." To him, as the covenant head and mediator of his people, it was given to have life in himself, that he might give eternal life to as many as the Father had given him. Christ possesses this life (John v. 26); Christ communicates it (John v. 25); Christ sustains it (John vi. 57); and Christ crowns it with eternal glory (John xvii. 24).

A peculiar characteristic of the life of God in the soul, is, that it is *concealed*. " Your life is *hid* with Christ in God." It is a hidden life. Its nature, its source, its actings, its supports, are veiled from the observation of men. "The world knoweth us not." It knew not Jesus when he dwelt in the flesh, else it would not have crucified the Lord of life and glory. Is it any wonder that it knows him not, dwelling, still deeper veiled, in the hearts of his members? It crucified Christ in his own person, it *has* crucified him in the persons of his saints, and, if power were given, would so crucify him yet again. And yet there is that in the divine life of the believer, which awakens the wonderment of a Christ-rejecting world. That the believer should be unknown, and yet well known; should die, and yet live; should be chastened, and yet not killed; sorrowful, yet always rejoicing; poor, yet making many rich; having nothing, and yet possessing all things, is indeed an enigma—a paradox to a carnal mind. Yea, there are moments when the believer is a mystery to *himself*. How the divine life in his soul is sustained in the midst of so much that enfeebles, kept alive surrounded by so much that deadens, the glimmering spark not extinguished, though obscured, amid the billows! To drop all figure,—how his soul advances when most opposed, soars when most burdened, rejoices when most afflicted, and sings the sweetest and the loudest, when the cross presses the heaviest, and the thorn pierces the deepest, may well cause him to exclaim, "I am a wonder to others, but a greater wonder to myself!" But, if the nature and the supports of the divine life in the soul are hid, not so are its *effects*, and these prove its existence and reality. The world has its keen, detecting eye upon the believer. It marks well his every step, it ponders narrowly his every going, it investigates and analyses closely his secret motives. No flaw, no deviation, no compromise, escapes its notice or its censure: it expects, and it has a right to expect, perfect harmony of principle and practice; it rebukes, and it has a right to rebuke, any marked discrepancy between the two. We say, then, that the *effects* of the life of God in the soul of the believer are observed by an ungodly world. There is that in the honest upright walk of a child of God, which arrests the attention and awakens the surprise of men, who, while they hate and despise, cannot but admire and marvel at it.

Yet another characteristic of the divine life in the soul, is its *security*. "Your life is hid *with Christ in God*." There, nothing can touch it: no power can destroy it. It is "hid with Christ," the beloved Son of the Father, the delight, the glory, the richest and most precious treasure of Jehovah: still more, it is "hid with Christ *in* God," in the hand, in the heart, in the all-sufficiency, yea, in the eternity of God. Oh the perfect security of the spiritual life of the believer! No power on earth or in hell can move it. It may be stormed by Satan, assaulted by corruption, scorned by men, and even in the moment of unbelief and in the hour of deep trial its exist-ence doubted by the believer himself; yet there it is, deep lodged in the eternity of God, bound up in the heart and with the existence of Jehovah, and no foe can destroy it. "As soon," says Charnock, "might Satan pull God out of heaven, undermine the security of Christ, and tear him from the bosom of the Father, as deprive the believer of his spiritual life, or destroy that principle of grace which God has im-planted in him." But a greater than Charnock has declared, "I give unto them eternal life; and they shall never perish, neither shall any man pluck them out of my hand." John x. 28. Let the sheep and the lambs of the "little flock" rejoice that the Shepherd lives, and that because he lives they shall live also. But we now pass to the consideration of the DE-CLENSION of this life in the soul.

By a state of *incipient declension*, we mean that decay of spiritual life and grace in the believer which marks its earliest and more concealed stage. It is latent and hidden, and there-fore the least suspected and the more dangerous. The painful process of spiritual disease may be advanced in the soul so secretly, so silently, and so unobservedly, that the subject of it may have lost much ground, may have parted with many graces and much vigour, and may have been beguiled into an alarming state of spiritual barrenness and decay, before even a suspicion of his real condition has been awakened in his breast. Like Samson, he may awaken out of his sleep, and say, " I will go out as at other times before, and shake myself. And he wist not that the Lord was departed from him." Judges xvi. 20. Or he may resemble Ephraim, of whom it is recorded, " Strangers have devoured his strength, and he knoweth it not; yea, grey hairs are here and there upon him, yet he knoweth it not." Hos. vii. 9. This is the state of the soul we are now to examine,—a state that has to do, not with the outward observation of men, but more especially and immediately with a holy and heart-searching God. In looking into the state of a backslider in heart, we may, in the first place, show what an incipient state of declension does *not* necessarily involve.

And first; it does not involve any alteration in the essential character of divine grace, but is a secret decay of the health, vigour, and exercise of that grace in the soul. As in the animal frame, the heart loses nothing of its natural function, when, through disease, it sends but a faint and languid pulsation through the system; so in the spiritual constitution of the believer, divine grace may be sickly, feeble, and inoperative, and yet retain its character and its properties. The pulse may beat faintly, but still it beats; the seed may not be fruitful, but it " liveth and abideth for ever "; the divine nature may be languid, but it can never assimilate or coalesce with any other, and must always retain its divinity untainted and unchanged. And yet, without changing its nature, divine grace may decline to an alarming extent in its power and exercise. It may be sickly, drooping, and ready to die; it may become so enfeebled through its decay, as to present an ineffectual resistance to the inroads of strong corruption; so low, that the enemy may ride rough-shod over it at his will; so inoperative and yielding, that sloth, worldliness, pride, carnality, and their kindred vices, may obtain an easy and unresisted conquest.

This decay of grace may be advancing, too, without any marked decline in the spiritual perception of the judgment, as to the beauty and fitness of spiritual truth. The loss of spiritual *enjoyment*, not of a spiritual *perception* of the loveliness and harmony of the truth, shall be the symptom that betrays the true condition of the soul. The judgment shall lose none of its light, but the heart much of its fervour; the truths of revelation, especially the doctrines of grace, shall occupy the same prominent position as to their value and beauty, and yet the influence of these truths may be scarcely felt. The *Word of God* shall be assented to; but as the instrument of sanctification, of abasement, of nourishment, the believer may be an almost utter stranger to it; yea, he must necessarily be so, while this process of secret declension is going forward in his soul.

This incipient state of declension may not involve any lowering of the standard of holiness; and yet there shall be no ascending of the heart, no reaching forth of the mind towards a practical conformity to that standard. The judgment shall acknowledge the divine law, as embodied in the life of Christ, to be the rule of the believer's walk; and yet to so low and feeble a state may vital godliness have declined in the soul, there shall be no panting after conformity to Christ, no breathing after holiness, no " resistance unto blood, striving against sin." Oh, it is an alarming condition for a Christian man, when the heart contradicts the judgment, and the life belies the profession!—when there is more *knowledge* of the truth than *experience* of its power,—more light in the understanding than grace in the affections,—more pretension in the profession than holiness and spirituality in the walk! And yet to this sad and melancholy state it is possible for a Christian professor to be reduced. How should it lead the man of empty notions, of mere creeds, of lofty pretension, of cold and lifeless orthodoxy, to pause, search his heart, examine his conscience, and ascertain the true state of his soul before God!

Once more: This state of secret departure from God may exist in connexion with an outward and rigid observance of the means of grace; and yet there shall be no spiritual use of, or enjoyment in, the means. And this, it may be, is the great lullaby of his soul. Rocked to sleep by a mere formal religion, the believer is beguiled into the delusion that his heart is right, and his soul prosperous in the sight of God. Even more than this,—a declining believer may have sunk so deeply into a state of formality, as to substitute the outward and the public means of grace for a close and secret walk with God. He may have taken up his abode in the outer courts of the temple; he may dwell in the mere porch of the sanctuary. Frequent or even occasional retirement consecrated to meditation, self-examination, the reading of God's word, and secret prayer, may yield to an outward, bustling form of godliness. Public and committee meetings—religious societies—business and professional engagements—wearing a religious aspect, and even important in their subordinate places, may thrust out God from the soul, and exclude Christ from the heart. And that a believer should be satisfied to "live at this poor dying rate," content to dwell amid the din and the bustle of the outworks, is one of the most palpable and alarming symptoms of the decline of the life of God in his soul. But let us group some of the more *positive* marks of an incipient and hidden state of spiritual declension.

When a professing man can proceed with his accustomed religious duties, strictly, regularly, formally, and yet experience no enjoyment of God in them, no filial nearness, no brokenness and tenderness, and no consciousness of sweet return, he may suspect that his soul is in a state of secret and incipient backsliding from God. Satisfying and feeding his soul—if feeding it may be called—with a lifeless form; what stronger symptom needs he of his real state? A healthy, growing state of religion in the soul demands more for its nourishment and support than this. A believer panting for God, hungering and thirsting after righteousness, grace thriving, the heart deeply engaged in spiritual duties, lively, prayerful, humble, and tender, ascending in its frame and desires,—a state marked by these features cannot be tied down to a lifeless, spiritless form of religious duties. These were but husks to a healthy state of the life of God in the soul. It wants more. It will hunger and thirst, and this spiritual longing must be met. And nothing can satisfy and satiate it but living upon Christ, the bread and the water of life. "I am the bread of life." "If any man thirst, let him come unto me and drink." "My flesh is meat indeed, and my blood is drink indeed." The professing man that goes all his days without this nourishment, thus starving his soul, may well exclaim, "My leanness, my leanness!" Oh, how solemn to such are the words of our Lord, "Verily, verily, I say unto you, Except ye eat the flesh of the Son of Man, and drink his blood, ye have no life in you." John vi. 53.

Again: When a professing man can read his Bible with no spiritual taste, or when he searches it, not with a sincere desire to know the mind of the Spirit in order to a holy and obedient walk, but with a merely curious, or literary taste and aim, it is a sure evidence that his soul is making but a retrograde movement in real spirituality. Nothing perhaps more strongly indicates the tone of a believer's spirituality, than the light in which the Scriptures are regarded by him. They may be read, and yet be read as any other book, without the deep and solemn conviction that "all scripture is given by inspiration of God, and is profitable for doctrine, for reproof, for correction, for instruction in righteousness; that the man of God may be perfect, thoroughly furnished unto all good works." 2 Tim. iii. 16, 17. They may be read without a spiritual relish, without being turned into prayer, without treasuring up in the heart and reducing to daily practice its holy precepts, its precious promises, its sweet consolations, its faithful warnings, its affectionate admonitions, its tender rebukes. And thus read, how can a believer expect to derive that "profit" from the Scriptures which they were intended, and are so calculated to convey?

When a professing Christian can *pray*, and yet acknowledge that he has no nearness to the throne, no touching of the sceptre, no fellowship with God,—calls him "Father," without the sense of adoption,—confesses sin in a general way, without any looking up to God through the cross,—has no consciousness of possessing the ear and the heart of God, the evidence is undoubted of a declining state of religion in the soul. And when too, he can find no sweetness in a *spiritual ministry*, —when he is restless and dissatisfied under a searching and practical unfolding of truth,—when the doctrines are preferred to the precepts, the promises to the commands, the consolations to the admonitions of the gospel, incipient declension is marked.

When the believer has but few dealings with Christ—his blood but seldom travelled to,—his fulness but little lived upon,—his love and glory scarcely mentioned, the symptoms of declension in the soul are palpable. Perhaps nothing forms a more certain criterion of the state of the soul than this. We would be willing to test a man's religion, both as to its nature and its growth, by his reply to the question, "What think ye of Christ?" Does his blood daily moisten the root of thy profession? Is his righteousness that which exalts thee out of and above thyself, and daily gives thee free and near access to God? Is the sweetness of his love much in thy heart, and the fragrance of his name much on thy lips? Are thy corruptions daily carried to his grace, thy guilt to his blood, thy trials to his heart? In a word, is Jesus the substance of thy life, the source of thy sanctification, the spring-head of thy joys, the theme of thy song, the one glorious object on which thine eye

is ever resting, the mark towards which thou art ever pressing? Be not offended, reader, if we remark, that a professing
man may talk well of Christ, and may do homage to his
name, and build up his cause, and promote his kingdom, and
yet rest short of having *Christ in his heart*, the hope of glory.
It is not the *talking about* religion, or ministers, or churches,
nor an outward zeal for their prosperity, that either constitutes or indicates a truly spiritual man. And yet how much
of this in our day passes current for the life of God in the
soul? Oh that among God's dear saints there were less talking of ministers, and more of Jesus; less of sermons, and more
of the power of the truth in their souls; less of " I am of Paul,"
and " I of Apollos," and more of " I am of Christ."

An uncharitable walk towards other Christians, marks a
low state of grace in the soul. The more entirely the heart is
occupied with the love of Christ, the less room will there be for
uncharitableness towards his saints. It is because there is so
little love to Jesus, that there is so little towards his followers.
In proportion as the mind becomes spiritual, it rises above
party distinctions and names,—it resigns its narrow and ex-
clusive views, casts away its prejudices against other sections
of the one church, and embraces in the yearnings of its Christian sympathy all who " love the Lord Jesus Christ in sincerity." In advocating a wider platform of Christian love, we
would by no means " sell the truth," or compromise principles, or immolate conscience upon the altar of an infidel
liberalism. But that for which we plead, is, more of that
Christian love, tender-heartedness, kindness, charity which
allows the right of private judgment, respects a conscientious
maintenance of truth, and concedes to others the same privilege it claims for itself. Differing as many of the saints of
God necessarily do in judgment, does the same necessity exist
wherefore they shall be alienated in affection? We think, far
from it. There is common ground on which all Christians
who hold the Head can stand. There are truths which can

assimilate all our minds, and blend all our hearts. Why then should we stand aloof from the one body and exclaim, " The temple of the Lord, the temple of the Lord are we?" Why should we refuse to recognise the Father's image in the children's face, and treat them as *aliens* in person, in spirit. and in language, because they see not eye to eye with us, in all our interpretations of God's word? Why should not " all bitterness, and wrath, and anger, and clamour, and evil speaking, be put away, with all malice?" and why should we not be " kind one to another, tender-hearted, forgiving one another, even as God for Christ's sake hath forgiven us," seeing that the church is but one, the family but one, that true believers are all " one in Christ Jesus "? This will be so where there is a deepening spirituality. And its absence marks a decay of grace, a waning of the life of God in the soul.

We have thus endeavoured to bring to view some of the prominent characteristics of a state of incipient declension of the life of God in the believer. It will be seen that we have referred to those only which mark the *hidden* departure of the heart from God;—that state that is so concealed, so veiled from the eye, and wearing so fair an exterior, that all suspicion of its existence is lulled to rest, and the soul is soothed with the delusion that all is well with it. Dear reader, is this *thy* state? Has this book thus far detected in thee any secret declension, any concealed departure, any heart backsliding? Has it proved to thee—the Spirit of God speaking by it—that thy soul is in an unhealthy state, the Divine life within thee is drooping? Turn not from the discovery, painful though it be. Look at it fully, honestly. It is no step towards the recovery of a sickly state, to disguise the worst symptoms of that state from the eye. The mark of true wisdom and skill is, to ascertain the worst of the disease, to probe the depth of the wound. And although such a course may be painful to he patient, it is essential to his thorough recovery. Beloved der, it is important that thou shouldst know the exact state of thy soul before God. And if thou art sincere in that petition which has often breathed from thy lip, "Search me, O God, and know my heart; try me, and know my thoughts; and see if there be any wicked way in me"; thou wilt thank him for any gentle and faithful admonition that sets thee upon the great work of self-examination. "It is fit," says Dr. Owen, "that professors of all sorts should be reminded of these things; for we may see not a few of them under visible decays, without any sincere endeavours after a recovery, who yet please themselves that the root of the matter is in them. It is so, if love of the world, conformity unto it, negligence in holy duties, and coldness in spiritual love, be an evidence of such decays. But let none deceive their own souls; wherever there is a saving principle of grace, it will be thriving and growing unto the end. And if it fall under obstructions, and thereby into decays for a season, it will give no rest or quietness unto the soul wherein it is, but will labour continually for a recovery. Peace in a spiritually-decaying condition, is a soul-ruining security; better be under terror on the account of surprisal into some sin, than be in peace under evident decays of spiritual life."

Some of the marked characteristics of the state of heart declension which we have been considering, are so strikingly set forth in the case of the church, as described by the Holy Ghost in the fifth chapter of the Song of Solomon, that we would direct the serious attention of the reader to it in connexion with this part of our work.

In the 2nd verse, *the church acknowledges her drowsy, yet not entirely insensible condition:* "I sleep, but my heart waketh." Here was the existence of the Divine life in the soul, and yet that life was on the decline. She knew that she had fallen into a careless and slumbering state, that the work of grace in her soul was decaying, that the spirit of slumber had come over her; but the awful feature was, *she was content to be so.* She heard her Beloved knock; but, so enam-

oured was she with her state of drowsiness, she gave no heed
to it—she opened not to him. " I sleep, but my heart waketh:
it is the voice of my Beloved that knocketh, saying, Open to
me, my sister, my love, my dove, my undefiled; for my head
is filled with dew, and my locks with the drops of the night."
Thus addressed, her duty would have been instantly to have
aroused herself from her sleep, and admitted her Lord. A believer may fall into a drowsy state of soul, not so profound as
to be entirely lost to the voice of his Beloved speaking by
conscience, by the word, and by providences: and yet so far
may his grace have decayed, so cold may his love have grown,
and so hardening may have been his declension, he shall be
content that this should be his state. O, alarming symptom
of soul declension, when the indulgence of sloth and self is
preferred to a visit from Jesus!

Then observe that, *when she did arise, Christ had withdrawn himself.* " I opened to my Beloved, but my Beloved
had withdrawn himself, and was gone: my soul failed when
he spake; I sought him, but I could not find him; I called
him, but he gave me no answer." Ver. 6. Weary with wait-
ing so long, grieved at the discovery he made of her deep
declension, and wounded by her cold repulse, he withdrew
his sensible, loving presence, and left her to the consequences
of her sad departure. The Lord never withdraws himself from
his people willingly: he is never actuated by an arbitrary impulse of his will. Such is his delight in his people, such his
love towards them, and such the joy he derives from their
fellowship, that he would walk with them all the day long,
and sun them with the unclouded light of his countenance.
But when he hides himself for a little moment, he is driven
from their embrace by their lukewarmness of heart, and unkind resistance of his love. Possessing a tender heart himself,
the slightest indifference discoverable in his child wounds it:
an ocean of love himself, the least lukewarmness in the love
of his people causes him to withdraw. And yet this momen-

tary withdrawment is not a judicial, but a fatherly, loving correction, to bring them to a knowledge and confession of their state: "I will go and return to my place, till they acknowledge their offence, and seek my face; in their affliction they will seek me early." Hos. v. 15.

It is worthy of remark, that *she receded into this state of declension immediately after a peculiar manifestation of Christ's love to her soul*. We find her thus inviting her Beloved: "Awake, O north wind, and come, thou south; blow upon my garden, that the spices may flow out. Let my Beloved come into his garden, and eat his pleasant fruits." He graciously accepts the invitation: "I am come into my garden, my sister, my spouse. I have gathered my myrrh with my spice; I have eaten my honeycomb with my honey; I have drunk my wine with my milk. Eat, O friends; drink, yea, drink abundantly, O beloved." Thus was her declension preceded by near and peculiar communion with her Lord. And how many of the Lord's people can testify to the same solemn truth, that some of their saddest departures have immediately followed seasons of the most endeared and holy fellowship with their God and Father! It is after such periods that the believer is most exposed to a spirit of self-complacency. Without great vigilance over the heart, self takes the glory and the praise of the gracious visit of love Jesus has made to the soul, and looks within for some secret cause of the mercy. When the Lord imparts a blessing, we need especial grace to keep us from falling through that very blessing. The case of the disciples affords a memorable illustration of this thought. The occasion on which the circumstance transpired to which we are about to refer, was a most solemn and affecting one; it was the scene that immediately preceded the crucifixion of Jesus. Luke thus records it: "And he took bread, and gave thanks, and brake it, and gave unto them, saying, This is my body which is given for you: this do in remembrance of me. Likewise also the cup after supper, saying, This cup is the new testament in my blood, which is shed for you." Luke xxii. 19, 20. What moment could have been more holy than this? what occasion more solemn and sacred? Here were the disciples holding fellowship with their adorable Immanuel in the awful mystery of his sufferings! But immediately after the close of this hallowed service, what do we read?—"There was also a strife among them, which should be accounted the greatest." Verse 24. Here were the worst exhibitions of fallen nature,—passion, hatred, envy, rankling in the heart, at a moment when the elements of their Saviour's dying love were yet upon their lips! Oh, what does this instructive lesson teach us!—trust not in frames and feelings, pray without ceasing, and particularly "watch unto prayer" immediately after seasons of peculiar nearness to God, or especial mercies received at his hands. "Special spiritual enjoyments," wisely remarks Traill, "are dangerous, and render a man very needy of the helping grace of God. They expose to special temptations, are apt to give rise to special corruptions, such as spiritual pride, contentedness with a present good condition, dullness of desire after a better state. If the Lord grant singular communications of himself, know that it is a season of special need of grace to guide them well. They would return more frequently, and would spring higher and last longer if they were better improved. The greater the blessing be, the greater the sin of its abuse; the greater the blessing be, the greater is the difficulty of guiding it well; and the more difficult the work, the greater our need of the grace of God; and the more frequent and fervent should our applications be to the throne of grace for that needful, helpful grace."

Yet once more: Mark *the hardening tendency of repeated declension* in her case. In chap. iii. 1, she manifests some desire for Christ, though her posture indicated a slothful spirit: "By night on my bed I sought him whom my soul loveth." Immediately after, Christ knocks, but she had sunk so deep in slumber that she arose not to admit him. Trace the steps, and mark the deadening nature of soul declension. She first places herself in the posture of sloth, and soon is heard to say, "I sleep." Why is it that so many who appear to be seeking Christ, rest short of him? It is not difficult in most cases to ascertain the true cause. It is this—they seek him in a slumbering posture—on their beds. Their desires are so languid, their frame of spirit so dead, their hearts so cold, that their very manner of seeking him seems to give an air of insincerity to their desires, and would seem to plead for a denial of their requests. Ponder again her confession:—Oh, is it not the confession of many?—"By night on my bed I sought him whom my soul loveth: I sought him, *but I found him not.*" And the reason why she found him not, was her slothful posture, and her drowsy spirit in seeking him! Guard against a slothful seeking of Jesus. With such a frame, disappointment will inevitably ensue. But seek him with all your heart, with all your desire, with the whole bent of your soul. Seek him as thy chief, thine only good. Seek him as that which can supply the absence of all other good, without whom nothing is good. Seek him as that blessing that can turn every bitter cup into sweetness, every dark cloud into brightness, every cross into a mercy; that can bring bread out of the eater, and honey out of the rock. Oh what a portion has that soul that has Jesus for its portion! "The Lord is my portion, saith my soul, therefore will I hope in him." But he must be sought with all the vigour of the soul, with all the intensity of desire, and with all perseverance of purpose, if he would be found. And well is he worth this labour of search. He is that pearl that will repay a diligent seeking. He will plentifully reward every sincere, humble comer. Not a want but he will supply, not a wound but he will heal, not a sorrow but he will soothe, not a sin but he will pardon, not a corruption but he will subdue. But seek him with full purpose of soul, and he shall be found. "When thou saidst, Seek ye my face, my

heart said unto thee, Thy face, Lord, *will* I seek." Ps. xxvii.
8. "The soul of the sluggard desireth, and hath nothing; but
the soul of the diligent shall be made fat." Prov. xiii. 4.

There is yet one more remarkable feature in the state of the
church we have been considering, too instructive to pass by
unnoticed;—we allude to the persuasion she felt, that though
the Divine life in her soul was at a low ebb, *still, Christ was
hers, and she was Christ's*. "I sleep, but my heart waketh;
it is the voice of my Beloved that knocketh." In the worst
frame that can affect a true child of God, there is always some
indication that the Divine life in the soul is not quite extinguished. In its greatest decay, there is yet some symptom of
life. In the darkest hour, there is that in the nature of true
grace, which emits some scintillation of its essential glory; in
its greatest defeat, that which asserts its divinity. Just as a
king, though deposed from his throne and driven into exile,
can never entirely divest himself of the dignity of his regal
character; so real grace, though often severely tried, sharply
assailed, and sometimes momentarily defeated, can never sink
its character, nor relinquish its sovereignty. Mark the proof
of this in the case of the apostle Paul: "Now then it is no
more I that do it, but sin that dwelleth in me. For the good
that I would I do not: but the evil which I would not, that I
do. Now if I do that I would not, it is no more I that do it,
but sin that dwelleth in me." Rom. vii. 17, 19, 20. And so
the church expresses it, "I sleep, *but* my heart waketh." In
her most drowsy, slothful state, she could not forget that she
was still her Beloved's, and that her Beloved was hers. Glorious nature, and blessed triumph of the life of God in the soul
of man!

We now come to the consideration of the REVIVAL of this
Divine life in the soul of the believer. From what has been
already advanced it will be perceived that we are far from
considering this a hopeless state. For a declining believer to
settle down under the conviction that such a state is *irrecover-*

able; that because he has taken the first step in departure from God, he must necessarily take the second, is to afford the most alarming evidence of a state of soul declension. But so far from this, we state it distinctly and emphatically, that whatever be the departure of a backsliding child of God, it is recoverable: not a step has he lost but may be retraced; not a grace has decayed but may be restored; not a joy has fled but may be won back. Alas! for us, when the day comes that shall close up every avenue to the return of a backsliding soul! that tells us that the Father no longer welcomes home the prodigal; that the blood of Jesus no longer heals a wounded spirit; that the Holy Ghost no longer restores the lost joys of God's salvation! But we desire now to show, that for every poor, self-condemned, heart-broken, returning soul, there is a lingering affection in the heart of the Father, a welcome in the blood of Jesus, and a restorative power in the operation of the Spirit, and therefore every *encouragement* to arise and come to God.

The first direction which we would give in the way of recovery is, *acquaint yourself thoroughly with the real state of your soul as before God*. As the first step in conversion was to know yourself to be a lost, helpless, condemned sinner; so now, in your *re-conversion* to God, you must know the exact state of your soul. Be honest with yourself; let there be a thorough, faithful examination of your spiritual condition; let all disguise be removed, the eye withdrawn from the opinion of men, and the soul shut in with God in a close scrutiny of its worst state. Your minister, your church, your friend, may know nothing of the secret state of your soul; they may not even suspect any hidden decline of grace, any incipient backsliding of heart from God. To their partial eye, the surface may be fair to look upon; to them your spiritual state may present the aspect of prosperity and fruitfulness; but the solemn question is between God and your own soul. You have to do with a God that judgeth not as man judgeth—by the outward appearance only—but who judgeth the heart. "I, the Lord, search the heart." The "backslider in heart" may deceive himself, he may deceive others, but God he cannot deceive. Seek then to know the real condition of your soul. Search and see what graces of the Spirit have declined, what fruits of the Spirit have decayed. My reader, this is a solemn and a great work we have set you upon, but it is necessary to your recovery. We would bring you into the court of your own bosom, to examine fairly and strictly the spiritual state of your soul. It is a solemn process! The *witnesses* summoned to testify are many;—conscience is a witness—how often it has been silenced; the word is a witness—how sadly it has been neglected; the throne of grace is a witness—how frequently it has been slighted; Christ is a witness—how much he has been undervalued; the Holy Spirit is a witness—how deeply he has been grieved; God is a witness—how greatly he has been robbed. All these testify against the soul of a backslider in heart, and yet all plead for its return!

The second step is, to *discover and bring to light the cause of the soul's declension.* "Is there not a cause?" Search and see what has fallen as a blight upon thy soul, what is feeding at the root of thy Christianity. The apostle Paul, skilful to detect, and faithful to reprove, any declension in the faith or laxity in the practice of the early churches, discovered in that of Galatia a departure from the purity of the truth, and a consequent carelessness in their walk. Grieved at the discovery, he addresses to them an affectionate and faithful epistle, expressive of his astonishment and pain, and proposing a solemn and searching inquiry. "I marvel," he writes, "that ye are so soon removed from him that called you into the grace of Christ. How, after that ye have known God, or rather are known of God, how turn ye again to the weak and beggarly elements? I am afraid of you, lest I have bestowed upon you labour in vain. Where is the blessedness ye spake of? I stand in doubt of you. Ye did run well; who did hinder you? This persuasion cometh not of him that calleth you." To the reader, conscious, as he hangs over this page, of secret declension in his soul, we propose the same searching and tender inquiry. Ye did run well; who did hinder you?—what stumbling-block has fallen in your way?—what has impeded your onward course?—what has enfeebled your faith, chilled your love, drawn your heart from Jesus, and lured you back to the weak and beggarly elements of a poor world? You set out fair; for a time you ran well; your zeal, and love, and humility, gave promise of a useful life, of a glorious race, and of a successful competition for the prize; but something has hindered. What is it? Is it the world, creature love, covetousness, ambition, presumptuous sin, unmortified corruption, the old leaven unpurged? *Search it out*. Rest not until it be discovered. Your declension is *secret*, perhaps the *cause* is *secret*, some spiritual duty secretly neglected, or some known sin secretly indulged. *Search it out*, and bring it to light. It must be a cause adequate to the production of effects so serious. You are not as you once were. Your soul has lost ground; the Divine life has declined; the fruit of the Spirit has withered; the heart has lost its softness, the conscience its tenderness, the mind its seclusion, the throne of grace its sweetness, the cross of Jesus its attraction. Oh, how sad and melancholy the change that has passed over you! And have you not the consciousness of it in your soul? Where is the blessedness ye spake of? where is the sunlight countenance of a reconciled Father? Where are the rich moments spent before the cross? the hallowed scenes of communion in the closet, shut in with God? Where is the voice of the turtledove, the singing of birds, the green pastures where thou didst feed, the still waters on whose banks thou didst repose? Is it *all* gone? Is it winter with thy soul? Ah! yes; thy soul is made to feel that it is an evil and a bitter thing to depart from the living God. But yet there is hope.

The next step in the work of personal revival, is, *to take the cause of the soul's declension immediately to the throne of grace, and lay it before the Lord.* There must be no parleying with it, no compromise, no concealment: there must be a full and unreserved disclosure before God, without aught of palliation or disguise. Let your sin be confessed in all its guilt, aggravation, and consequences. This is just what God loves—an open, ingenuous confession of sin. Searching and knowing, though he does, all hearts, he yet delights in the honest and minute acknowledgment of sin from his backsliding child. Language cannot be too humiliating, the detail cannot be too minute. Mark the stress he has laid upon this duty, and the blessing he has annexed to it. Thus he spake to the children of Israel, that wandering, backsliding, rebellious people: " If they shall *confess* their iniquity, and the iniquity of their fathers, with their trespass which they trespassed against me, and that also they have walked contrary unto me; and that I also have walked contrary unto them, and have brought them into the land of their enemies; if then their uncircumcised hearts be humbled, and they then accept of the punishment of their iniquity; then will I remember my covenant with Jacob, and also my covenant with Isaac, and also my covenant with Abraham will I remember; and I will remember the land." Levit. xxvi. 40-42. Truly may we exclaim, " Who is a God like unto thee, that pardoneth iniquity, and passeth by the transgression of the remnant of his heritage! he retaineth not his anger for ever, because he delighteth in mercy." This, too, was the blessed experience of David, God's dear yet often backsliding child: " I *acknowledged* my sin unto thee, and mine iniquity have I not hid. I said, I will *confess* my transgressions unto the Lord: and thou *forgavest* the iniquity of my sin." Psalm xxxii. 5. And how did the heart of God melt with pity and compassion when he heard the audible relentings of his Ephraim! " I have surely heard Ephraim bemoaning himself thus: Thou hast chastised me, and I was chastised, as a bullock unaccustomed to the yoke: turn thou me, and I shall be turned; for thou art the Lord my God." And what was the answer of God! "Is Ephraim my dear son? is he a pleasant child? for since I spake against him, I do earnestly remember him still; therefore my bowels are troubled for him: I will surely have mercy upon him, saith the Lord." Jer. xxxi. 18, 20. Nor is the promise of pardon annexed to confession of sin, unfolded with less clearness and consolatoriness in the New Testament writings. "If we *confess* our sins, he is faithful and just to *forgive* us our sins, and to cleanse us from all unrighteousness." 1 John i. 9. How full, then, the blessing, how rich the consolation connected with an honest, heartbroken confession of sin? How easy and how simple, too, this method of return to God! "Only acknowledge thine iniquity." Jer. iii. 13. It is but a confession of sin over the head of Jesus, the great sacrifice for sin. O, *what* is this that God says? "*Only* acknowledge thine iniquity!" Is this *all* he requires of his poor wandering child? This is all! "Then," may the poor soul exclaim, "Lord, I come to thee. I am a backslider, a wanderer, a prodigal. I have strayed from thee like a lost sheep. My love has waxed cold, my steps have slackened in the path of holy obedience; my mind has yielded to the corrupting, deadening influence of the world, and my affections have wandered in quest of other and earthly objects of delight. But, behold, I come unto thee. Dost thou invite me? Dost thou stretch out thy hand? Dost thou bid me approach thee? Dost thou say, 'Only acknowledge thine iniquity?' Then, Lord, I come; in the name of thy dear Son, I come; 'restore unto me the joy of thy salvation.'" Thus confessing sin over the head of Jesus, until the heart has nothing more to confess but the sin of its confession—for, beloved reader, our very confession of sin needs to be confessed over, our very tears need to be wept over, and our very prayers need to be prayed over, so defaced with sin is all that we do—the soul, thus emptied and unburthened, is prepared to receive anew the seal of a Father's forgiving love.

The true posture of a returning soul is beautifully presented to view in the prophecy of Hosea, xiv. 1, 2: "O Israel, return unto the Lord thy God; for thou hast fallen by thine iniquity. Take with you words, and turn to the Lord: say unto him, Take away all iniquity, and receive us graciously: so will we render thee the calves [sacrifices] of our lips." Here are conviction, godly sorrow, humiliation, and confession, the essential elements of a true return to God. Conviction of the true state of the declining soul; godly sorrow resulting from the discovery; humiliation, deep and sincere, on account of it; and a full and unreserved confession of it before God. O blessed evidences! O lovely posture of a restored soul!

Essentially connected with the discovery and the confession, there must be *the entire mortification and abandonment of the cause* of the soul's secret declension. Apart from this, there can be no true revival of the work of Divine grace in the heart. The true spiritual mortification of indwelling sin, and the entire forsaking of the known cause, whatever it is found to be, of the heart's declension, constitute the true elements of a believer's restoration to the joys of God's salvation. And when we speak of the mortification of sin, let not the nature of this sacred work be misunderstood. It *has* been in the case of many, why may it not in yours? There may exist all the surface-marks of mortification, and still the heart remain a stranger to the work. An awakening sermon, an alarming providence, or a startling truth, may for a moment arrest and agitate the backsliding soul. There may be an opening of the eyelid, a convulsive movement of the spiritual frame, which, to a superficial observer, may wear the appearance of a real return to consciousness, of a true waking up to new life and vigour of the slumbering soul, and yet these may be but the transient and fitful impulses of a sickly and a drowsy spirit. The means of grace, too, may be returned to—the secret declension felt, deplored and acknowledged, but the hidden *cause* remaining unmortified and unremoved, all appearance of recovery quickly and painfully subsides. It was but a transient, momentary shock, and all was still; the heavy eyelid but feebly opened, and closed again; the "goodness" that promised so fair, was but as the morning cloud and the early dew. And the reason is found in the fact, that *there was no true mortification of sin*. And so I may repair to a plant withering and drooping in my garden; I may employ every external means for its revival; I may loosen the earth about it, water, and place it in the warm sunbeam; but if the while I had not discovered and removed the hidden cause of its decay—if I had not known that a worm was secretly feeding at the root, and, in ignorance of this, had proceeded with my surface-work of restoration, what marvel, though the morning sunbeam, and the evening dew, and the loosened earth, had produced a momentary freshness and life, that yet my plant had ceased to exist, had withered and died? Thus may it be with a declining believer. The external means of revival may be sedulously employed, means of grace diligently used and even multiplied, but all to no real and permanent effect, while a worm secretly feeds at the root; and until the hidden cause of decay be mortified, removed, and utterly extirpated, the surface revival does but end in a profounder sleep, and a more fearful deception of the soul. Again, and yet again would we repeat it—there cannot possibly be any true, spiritual, and abiding revival of grace in a believer, while *secret sin* remains undiscovered and unmortified in the heart. True and spiritual mortification of sin is not a surface-work: it consists not merely in pruning the dead tendrils that hang here and there upon the branch; it is not the lopping off of outward sins, and an external observance of spiritual duties; it includes essentially far more than this: it is a laying the axe at the *root* of sin in the believer; it aims at nothing less than the complete subjection of the *principle* of sin; and until this is effectually done, there can be no true return of the heart to God. Christian reader, what is the cause of thy soul's secret declension? What is it that at this moment feeds upon the precious plant of grace, destroying its vigour, its beauty, and its fruitfulness? Is it an inordinate attachment to the creature? *mortify it;*—the love of self? *mortify it;*—the love of the world? *mortify it;*—some sinful habit secretly indulged? *mortify it.* It must be mortified, *root* as well as branch, if you would experience a thorough return to God. Dear though it be, as a right hand, or as a right eye, if yet it comes between thy soul and God, if it crucifies Christ in thee, if it weakens faith, enfeebles grace, destroys the spirituality of the soul, rendering it barren and unfruitful, rest not short of its utter mortification.

Nor must this great work be undertaken in your own strength. It is pre-eminently the result of God the Holy Ghost working in, and blessing the self-efforts of the believer: " If ye through the Spirit do mortify the deeds of the body, ye shall live." Rom. viii. 13. Here is a recognition of the believer's own exertions, in connexion with the power of the Holy Ghost: " If *ye*" (believers, ye saints of God) "*through the Spirit* do mortify the deeds of the body," &c. It is the work of the believer himself, but the power is of the Spirit of God. Take, then, your discovered sin to the Spirit: that Spirit, bringing the cross of Jesus, with a killing, crucifying power, into your soul, giving you such a view of a Saviour suffering for sin, as it may be you never had before, will in a moment lay your enemy slain at your feet. O yield not to despair, distressed soul! Art thou longing for a gracious revival of God's work within thee?—art thou mourning in secret over thy heart-declension?—hast thou searched and discovered the hidden cause of thy decay?—and is thy real desire for its mortification? Then look up, and hear the consolatory words of thy Lord: " I am the Lord that healeth thee." Exod. xv. 26. The Lord is thy healer; his love can restore thee; his blood can heal thee; his grace can subdue thy sin. "Take with you words, and turn to the Lord; say unto him, Take away all iniquity, and receive us graciously": and the Lord will answer, "I will heal their backslidings, I will love them freely; for mine anger is turned away from him."

Endeavour to enrich and enlarge your mind with more spiritual apprehensions of the personal glory, love, and fulness of Christ. All soul-declension arises from the admission of things into the mind contrary to the nature of indwelling grace. The world,—its pleasures, its vanities, its cares, its varied temptations,—these enter the mind, disguised in the shape often of lawful undertakings and duties, and draw off the mind from God, and the affections from Christ. These, too, weaken and deaden faith and love, and every grace of the indwelling Spirit: they are the "foxes that spoil the vines, for our vines have tender grapes." Sol. Song ii. 15. The world is a most hurtful snare to the child of God. It is impossible that he can maintain a close and holy walk with God, live as a pilgrim and a sojourner, wage a constant and successful warfare against his many spiritual foes, and at the same time open his heart to admit the greatest foe to grace—the love of the world. But when the mind is pre-occupied by Christ, filled with contemplations of his glory and grace and love, no room is left for the entrance of external allurements: the world is shut out, and the creature is shut out, and the fascinations of sin are shut out; and the soul holds a constant and undisturbed fellowship with God, while it is enabled to maintain a more vigorous resistance to every external attack of the enemy. And O, how blessed is the soul's communion, thus shut in with Jesus! "Behold, I stand at the door and knock: if any man hear my voice and open the door, I will come in to him, and will sup with him, and he with me." "I would come in," says the dear Lamb of God, "and dwell in you, and take up my abode with you, and sup with you, and you with me." This is true fellowship! And O, sweet response of his own Spirit in the heart, when the believing soul exclaims,—"When thou saidst, Seek ye my face; my heart said unto thee, Thy face, Lord, will I seek!" "Enter, thou precious Jesus; I want none but Thee; I desire no company, and would hear no voice but thine; I will have fellowship with none but thee,—let me sup with thee: yea, give me thine own flesh to eat, and thine own blood to drink." Ah! dear Christian reader, it is because we have so little to do with Jesus—we admit him so seldom and so reluctantly to our hearts—we have so few dealings with him—travel so seldom to his blood and righteousness, and live so little upon his fulness, that we are compelled so often to exclaim,—"My leanness, my leanness!" But, if we be "risen with Christ, seek those things which are above, where Christ sitteth on the right hand of God"; let us seek to know Christ more, to have more spiritual and enlarged comprehensions of his glory, to drink deeper into his love, to imbibe more of his Spirit, and conform more closely to his example.

But that which forms the great secret of all personal revival is yet to be disclosed; we allude *to a fresh baptism of the Holy Ghost.* This a declining soul needs more than all beside. Possessing this in a large degree, he possesses every spiritual blessing: it includes, and is the pledge of every other. Our dear Lord sought to impress this, his last consoling doctrine, upon the drooping minds of his disciples: his bodily presence in their midst, he taught them, was not to be compared with the spiritual and permanent dwelling of the Spirit among them. The descent of the Holy Ghost was to bring all things that he had taught them to their remembrance; it was to perfect them in their knowledge of the supreme glory of his person, the infinite perfection of his work, the nature and spirituality of his kingdom, and its ultimate and certain triumphs in the earth. The descent of the Spirit, too, was to mature them in personal holiness, and more eminently fit them for their arduous and successful labour in his cause, by deepening their spirituality, enriching them with more grace, and enlarging them with more love. And fully did the baptism of the Holy Ghost, on the day of Pentecost, accomplish all this: the apostles emerged from his influence, like men who had passed through a state of re-conversion.

And this is the state, dear reader, *you* must pass through, would you experience a revival of God's work in your soul: you must be *reconverted*, and that through a fresh baptism of the Holy Ghost. Nothing short of this will quicken your dying graces, and melt your frozen love; nothing save this will arrest your secret declension, and restore your backsliding heart. *You must be baptized afresh with the Spirit;* that Spirit whom you have so often and so deeply wounded, grieved, slighted and quenched, must enter you anew, and seal, and sanctify, and reconvert you. O arise, and pray, and agonize for the outpouring of the Spirit upon your soul; give up your lifeless religion, your form without the power, your prayer without communion, your confessions without brokenness, your zeal without love. And O, what numerous and precious promises cluster in God's word, all inviting you to seek this blessing! "He shall come down like rain upon the mown grass; as showers that water the earth." Psalm lxxii. 6. "I will heal their backslidings, I will love them freely; for mine anger is turned away from him. I will be as the dew unto Israel: he shall grow as the lily, and cast forth his roots as Lebanon. His branches shall spread, and his beauty shall be as the olive-tree, and his smell as Lebanon. They that dwell under his shadow shall return; they shall revive as the corn, and grow as the vine: the scent thereof shall be as the wine of Lebanon." Hos. xiv. 4-7. "Come, let us return unto the Lord; for he hath torn, and he will heal us; he hath smitten, and he will bind us up. After two days will he revive us, in the third day he will raise us up, and we shall live in his sight. Then shall we know, if we follow on to know the Lord: his going forth is prepared as the morning; and he shall come unto us as the rain, as the latter and former rain unto the earth. Hos. vi. 1-3. Seek, then, above and beyond all other blessings, the renewed baptism of the Holy Ghost. " Be filled with the Spirit "; seek it *earnestly*,—seek it under the deep conviction of your absolute *need of it*,—seek it *persever-ingly*,—seek it *believingly*. God has promised, " I will pour out my Spirit upon you "; and, asking it in the name of Jesus, you *shall* receive.

One word more: Be not surprised if the Lord should place you in circumstances of *deep trial*, in order to recover you from your soul-declension: the Lord often adapts the pecu-liarity of the discipline to that of the case. Is it *secret* de-clension? He may send some *secret rebuke*, some secret cross, some hidden chastisement; no one has discovered thy concealed declension, and no one discovers thy concealed correction. The declension was between God and thy soul, so also it may be is the rebuke; the backsliding was of the heart, so also is the chastisement. But if the sanctified trial works the recovery of your soul, the restoration to Christ of your wavering heart, the revival of his entire work within you, you shall adore him for the discipline; and with David, extolling the dealings of a covenant God and Father, shall exclaim,—" Before I was afflicted I went astray, but now have I kept thy word. It is good for me that I have been afflicted, that I might learn thy statutes!"

Lastly: Set out afresh for God and heaven, as though you had never started in the way before. Commence at the be-ginning; go as a sinner to Jesus; seek the quickening, healing, sanctifying influence of the Spirit; and let this be your prayer, presented, and urged until answered, at the footstool of mercy: "O Lord, revive thy work! Quicken me, O Lord! Restore unto me the joy of thy salvation!" In answer to thy petition, "He shall come down like rain upon the mown grass; as showers that water the earth "; and thy song shall be that of the church, "My Beloved spake, and said unto me,

Rise up, my love, my fair one, and come away. For lo, the winter is past, the rain is over and gone. The flowers appear on the earth, the time of the singing of birds is come, and the voice of the turtle is heard in our land. The fig-tree putteth forth her green figs, and the vines with the tender grape give a good smell. Arise, my love, my fair one, and come away."

CHAPTER II

DECLENSION IN LOVE

" The love of many shall wax cold."—Matt. xxiv. 12.

HAVING described the hidden and incipient declension of the believer, we propose in the present and succeeding chapters, to trace this melancholy state in some of its more advanced stages, as it is seen in the languor and decay of the graces of the Spirit in the soul. It is no longer the concealed, but *developed*, character of spiritual and personal declension that we are now to consider. Its type is more marked, and its symptoms more palpable and visible to the eye. It has arrived at such a stage as to render concealment impossible. Just as in the physical frame, a slight sinking in the heart's pulsation, even though the seat of disease is invisible, may be traced in the external symptoms that ensue; so, in the spiritual man, when there is a secret unhealthiness of soul, the effects are so marked in their character as to leave no doubt of its existence. The man may not himself be sensible of his backsliding state; he may wrap himself up in the fearful deception that all is well, close his eyes voluntarily against his real state, disguise from himself the rapidly advancing disease, crying " peace, peace," and putting far off the evil day; but with a spiritual and advancing believer, one whose eye is keen to detect an unfavourable symptom, and whose touch is skilful to mark a sickly pulse, the case is involved in no mystery.

In tracing the declension of some of the essential and prominent graces of the Spirit, we commence with the grace of LOVE, it constituting the spring-head of all the kindred graces. The spiritual state of the soul, and the vigour and promptness of its obedience, will correspond with the state and tone of the believer's affections towards God. If decay, coldness, declension, exist here, it is felt and traced throughout the entire obedience of the new man. Every grace of the Spirit feels it; every call to duty feels it; and every throb of the spiritual pulse will but betray the secret and certain declension of Divine love in the soul. Let the Christian reader, then, imagine what must be the spiritual unhealthiness of the believer, what his outward and visible declensions from God, when love, the spring of all spiritual duties, ceases to exert a vigorous influence, and when, as the heart of experimental godliness, it transmits but sickly and sluggish streams of life throughout the spiritual system. Let us, before we proceed to the immediate discussion of the main subject before us, present a brief and scriptural view of the necessity, nature, and operation of Divine love in the soul.

Love to God is spoken of in his word, as forming the primary and grand requirement of the Divine law. Thus is the truth declared, " Thou shalt love the Lord thy God with all thy heart, and with all thy soul, and with all thy mind. This is the first and great commandment." Matt. xxii. 37, 38. Now, it was both infinitely wise and good in God, thus to present himself the proper and lawful object of love. We say it was *wise*, because, had he placed the object of supreme affection lower than himself, it had been to have elevated an inferior object above himself. For whatever other object than God is loved with a sole and supreme affection, it is a deifying of that object, so that it, as God, sitteth in the temple of God, showing itself that it is God. It was *good*, because a lesser object of affection could never have met the desires and aspirations of an immortal mind. God has so constituted man, implanting in him such a capacity for happiness, and such boundless and immortal desires for its possession, as can find their full enjoyment only in infinity itself. He never designed that the intelligent and immortal creature should sip its bliss at a lower fountain than himself. Then it was infinitely wise and good in God, that he should have presented himself as the sole object of supreme love and worship to his intelligent creatures. His *wisdom* saw the necessity of having one centre of supreme and adoring affection, and one object of supreme and spiritual worship to angels and to men. His *goodness* suggested that that centre and that that object should be *himself*, the perfection of infinite excellence, the fountain of infinite good. That, as from him went forth all the streams of life to all creatures, it was but reasonable and just that to him should return, and in him should centre, all the streams of love and obedience of all intelligent and immortal creatures: that, as he was the most intelligent, wise, glorious, and beneficent object in the universe, it was meet that the first, strongest, and purest love of the creature should soar towards, and find its resting-place in him.

Love to God, then, forms the grand requirement, and fundamental precept of the Divine law. It is binding upon all intelligent beings. From it no consideration can release the creature. No plea of inability, no claim of inferior objects, no opposition of rival interest, can lessen the obligation of every creature that hath breath to " love the Lord his God with all his heart, and with all his soul, and with all his mind." It grows out of the relation of the creature to God, as his Creator, Moral Governor, and Preserver; and as being in himself the only object of infinite excellence, wisdom, holiness, majesty, and grace. This obligation, too, to love God with supreme affection, is binding upon the creature irrespective of any advantage which may result to him from so loving God. It is most true that God has benevolently connected supreme happiness with supreme love, and has threatened supreme misery, where supreme affection is withheld; yet, independent of any blessing that may accrue to the creature from its love to God, the infinite excellence of the Divine nature, and the eternal relation in which he stands to the intelligent universe, render it irreversibly obligatory on every creature to love him with a supreme, paramount, holy, and unreserved affection.

Love, too, is the great *influential principle of the Gospel*. The religion of Jesus is pre-eminently a religion of motive : it excludes every compulsory principle; it arrays before the mind certain great and powerful motives with which it enlists the understanding, the will, and the affections, in the active service of Christ. Now the law of Christianity is not the law of coercion, but of love. This is the grand lever, the great influential motive,—" the love of Christ constraineth us." This was the apostle's declaration, and this his governing motive; and the constraining love of Christ is to be the governing motive, the influential principle of every believer. Apart from the constraining influence of Christ's love in the heart, there cannot possibly be a willing, prompt, and holy obedience to his commandments. A conviction of duty and the influence of fear may sometimes urge forward the soul, but love alone can prompt to a loving and holy obedience; and all obedience that springs from an inferior motive is not the obedience that the gospel of Jesus inculcates. The relation in which the believer stands to God, under the new covenant dispensation, is not that of a slave to his master, but of a child to its father. " And because ye are sons, God hath sent forth the Spirit of his Son into your hearts, crying, Abba, Father." Gal. iv. 6. " The Spirit itself beareth witness with our spirit, that we are the children of God." Rom. viii. 16. "Wherefore thou art no more a servant (a slave), but a son." Gal. iv. 7. With this new and spiritual relation, we look for a new and spiritual motive, and we find it in that single but comprehensive word—LOVE. And thus has our Lord declared it :

"If ye love me, keep my commandments." John xiv. 15. "If a man love me, he will keep my words; and he that loveth me not, keepeth not my sayings." Ver. 23, 24. It is then only where this love is shed abroad in the heart by the Holy Ghost, that we may expect to find the fruit of obedience. Swayed by this Divine principle, the believer labours not *for* life, but *from* life: not *for* acceptance, but *from* acceptance. A holy, self-denying, cross-bearing life, is not the drudgery of a slave, but the filial, loving obedience of a child: it springs from love to the person, and gratitude for the work of Jesus; and is the blessed effect of the spirit of adoption in the heart.

It must be acknowledged, too, that this motive is the most holy and influential of all motives of obedience. Love, flowing from the heart of Jesus into the heart of a poor, believing sinner, expelling selfishness, melting coldness, conquering sinfulness, and drawing that heart up in a simple and unreserved surrender, is, of all principles of action, the most powerful and sanctifying. Under the constraining influence of this principle, how easy becomes every cross for Jesus!—how light every burthen, how pleasant every yoke! Duties become privileges—difficulties vanish—fears are quelled—shame is humbled—delay is rebuked; and, all on flame for Jesus, the pardoned, justified, adopted child exclaims, "Here, Lord, am I, a living sacrifice; thine for time, and thine for eternity!"

Love is that principle that expels all legal fear from the heart. "There is no fear in love; but perfect love casteth out fear, because fear hath torment. He that feareth is not made perfect in love." 1 John iv. 18. Who that has felt it will deny that "fear hath torment?" The legal fear of death, of judgment, and of condemnation,—the fear engendered by a slavish view of the Lord's commandments,—a defective view of the believer's relation to God,—imperfect conceptions of the finished work of Christ,—unsettled apprehensions of the great fact of acceptance,—yielding to the power of unbelief,—

the retaining of guilt upon the conscience, or the influence of any concealed sin, will fill the heart with the torment of fear. Some of the most eminent of God's people have thus been afflicted: this was Job's experience,—" I am *afraid* of all my sorrows." " Even when I remember, I am *afraid*, and trembling taketh hold on my flesh." " When I consider him, I am *afraid* of him." So also David,—" What time I am *afraid*, I will trust in thee." " My flesh trembleth for *fear* of thee; I am *afraid* of thy judgments." But " perfect love casteth out fear ": he that feareth is not perfected in the love of Christ. The design and tendency of the love of Jesus shed abroad in the heart, is to lift the soul out of all its " bondage through fear of death " and its ultimate consequences, and soothe it to rest on that glorious declaration, triumphing in which many have gone to glory, " There is therefore now no condemnation to them which are in Christ Jesus." See the blessed spring from whence flows a believer's victory over all bondage-fear—from Jesus: not from his experience of the truth, not from evidence of his acceptance and adoption, not from the work of the Spirit in his heart, blessed as it is, but from out of, and away from, himself, even from Jesus. The blood and righteousness of Christ, based upon the infinite dignity and glory of his person, and wrought into the experience of the believer by the Holy Ghost, expel from the heart all fear of death and of judgment, and fill it with perfect peace. O thou of fearful heart! why these anxious doubts, why these tormenting fears, why this shrinking from the thought of death, why these distant, hard, and unkind thoughts of God? Why this prison-house,—why this chain? Thou art not perfected in the love of Jesus, for " perfect love casteth out fear "; thou art not perfected in that great truth, that Jesus is mighty to save, that he died for a poor sinner, that his death was a perfect satisfaction to Divine justice; and that without a single meritorious work of thine own, just as thou art, poor, empty, vile, worthless, unworthy, thou art welcome to the rich provision of sovereign grace and dying love. The simple belief of this will perfect thy heart in love; and perfected in love, every bondage-fear will vanish away. O seek to be perfected in Christ's love! It is a fathomless ocean. Why then shouldst thou not descend into it? Approach, for it is free; drink, for it is deep; launch into it, for it is broad. "The Lord direct your heart into the love of God."

Love is that grace of the Spirit that brings faith into active exercise; "faith which worketh by love," Gal. v. 6; and faith thus brought into exercise, brings every spiritual blessing into the soul. A believer stands by faith, Rom. xi. 20; he walks by faith, 2 Cor. v. 7; he overcomes by faith, 1 John v. 4; he lives by faith, Gal. ii. 20. Love is therefore a labouring grace; "God is not unrighteous to forget your work and labour of love, which ye have shewed towards his name." Heb. vi. 10. There is nothing indolent in the nature of true love; it is not an inert, sluggish principle: where it dwells in the heart in a healthy and vigorous state, it constrains the believer to live not to himself, but unto Him who loved and gave himself for him; it awakes the soul to watchfulness, sets it upon the work of frequent self-examination, influences it to prayer, daily walking in the precepts, acts of kindness, benevolence, and charity, all springing from love to God, and flowing in a channel of love to man.

The Holy Ghost distinguishes love as a part of the Christian armour: "Let us, who are of the day, be sober, putting on the breast-plate of faith and *love*." 1 Thess. v. 8. Without ardent and increasing love to God, the believer is but poorly armed against his numerous spiritual and ever-aggressive foes: but what a breast-plate and helmet is this in the day of battle! Who can overcome a child of God whose heart is overflowing with Divine love? what enemy can prevail against him thus armed? There is something so shielding in its influence, so repelling to the spirit of enmity and darkness, so obnoxious to sin, that he only is fit for the conflict who is well clad in the breast-plate of love. He may be, and he is, in himself, nothing but weakness; his foes many and mighty; hemmed in on every side by his spiritual Philistines; and yet, his heart soaring to God in love, longing for his presence, panting for his precepts, desiring above and beyond all other blessings, Divine conformity! O with what a panoply is he clothed! No weapon formed against him shall prosper: every "fiery dart of the adversary" shall be quenched, and he shall "come off more than a conqueror through Him who hath loved him."

In a word, love is immortal; it is that grace of the Spirit that will never die. This is not so with all the kindred graces; the period will come when they will no more be needed. The day is not far distant, when *faith* will be turned to sight, and *hope* will be lost in full fruition, but *love* will never die; it will live on, and expand the heart, and tune the lip, and inspire the song, through the unceasing ages of eternity. "Whether there be prophecies, they shall fail; whether there be tongues, they shall cease; whether there be knowledge, it shall vanish away"; but *love* never faileth; it is an eternal spring, welled in the bosom of Deity; heaven will be its dwelling-place, God its source, the glorified spirit its subject, and eternity its duration.

For one moment let the Christian reader call to mind the period and the circumstances of his *first espousals* to Jesus. If there ever was a blissful period of thy life,—if a spot of verdure in the remembrance of the past, on which the sunlight ever rests,—was it not the time, and is it not the place, where thy heart first expanded with the love of Jesus? Thou hast, it may be, trod many a thorny path since then; thou hast travelled many a weary step of thy pilgrimage—hast buffeted many storms, hast waded through many deep afflictions, and fought many severe battles,—but all have well-nigh faded from thy memory; but the hour and the events of thy "first love,"—these thou never hast forgotten, thou never canst forget. O ever to be loved, ever to be remembered with deep songs of joy, with adoring gratitude to free and sovereign grace, the period when the chains of thy bondage were broken,—when thy fettered soul broke from its thraldom, and sprang into the liberty of the sons of God,—when light discovered thy darkness, and that darkness rolled away before its increasing lustre,—when the Spirit wounded thee, then healed that wound with the precious balm of Gilead,—when he gave thee sorrow, then soothed that sorrow by a view of the crucified Lamb of God,—when faith took hold of Jesus, and brought the blessed assurance into the soul, "I am my beloved's, and my beloved is mine"; and when Jesus whispered,—O how tender was his voice!—"Thy sins, which were many, are all forgiven; go in peace." Blissful moment! How fresh is the whole transaction to thy mind: the sanctuary where thou didst worship,—the minister whom thou didst hear,—the people with whom thou didst associate,—the spot where thou didst lose thy burden, and where light, and love, and joy, broke in upon thy soul,—the saints who rejoiced over thee, and the happy converts who clustered around thee, mingling their joys and their songs with thine; and the man of God who introduced thee within the pale, and to the ordinances and the privileges of the Church of Christ,—all, all is now before thee with a vividness and a freshness as though it had but just transpired. O that the Lord should ever have reason to prefer the charge, "thou hast left thy first love!" And yet to the consideration of this melancholy state of a professing soul we have now to turn. May the Spirit of truth and of love be our guide and teacher!

The subject now before us for reflection, is the humbling and affecting truth, that *the grace of love in a child of God may greatly and sadly decline.* We speak, let it be remembered, not of the destruction of the principle, but of the decline of its power. This spiritual and influential truth cannot be too frequently nor too strongly insisted upon,—that though faith, and love, and hope, and zeal, and their kindred graces, may greatly decline in their vigour, fervour, and real growth; yet that they may entirely fail even in their greatest decay, or severest trial, the Word of God assures us can never be. To believe the opposite of this, is to deny their Divine origin, their spiritual and immortal character, and to impeach the wisdom, power, and faithfulness of God. Not a grain of the true wheat can ever be lost in the sifting, not a particle of the pure gold in the refining. Let us now be understood as unfolding in this chapter the declension of love in its vital actings in the soul, and in its influential character upon the outward, holy walk of a child of God.

In looking into God's Word, we find this to have been the solemn charge which he brought against his ancient professing people: "Thus saith the Lord, I remember thee, the kindness of thy youth, the love of thine espousals, when thou wentest after me in the wilderness, in a land that was not sown." Then follows the charge of declension in their love: "Thus saith the Lord, What iniquity have your fathers found in me, that they are gone far from me, and have walked after vanity, and are become vain?" "O generation, see ye the word of the Lord. Have I been a wilderness unto Israel? a land of darkness? Wherefore say my people, We are lords; we will come no more unto thee? Can a maid forget her ornaments, or a bride her attire? yet my people have forgotten me days without number." Jer. ii. 2, 5, 31. And to the same state, as forming an evidence of approaching desolations, our dear Lord refers, when He says, "And because iniquity shall abound, the love of many shall wax cold." Matt. xxiv. 12. And against the church of Ephesus the same charge is thus preferred: "Nevertheless I have somewhat against thee, because thou hast left thy first love." Rev. ii. 4. The following may be considered as forming some of the marked characteristics of the decay and declension of this principle.

When God becomes less an object of fervent desire, holy delight, and frequent contemplation, we may suspect a declension of Divine love in the soul. Our spiritual views of God, and our spiritual and constant delight in him, will be materially affected by the state of our spiritual love. If there is coldness in the affections, if the mind grows earthly, carnal, and selfish, dark and gloomy shadows will gather round the character and the glory of God. He will become less an object of supreme attachment, unmingled delight, adoring contemplation, and filial trust. The moment the supreme love of Adam to God declined,—the instant that it swerved from its proper and lawful centre, he shunned converse with God, and sought to embower himself from the presence of the Divine glory. Conscious of a change in his affections,—sensible of a divided heart, of subjection to a rival interest,—and knowing that God was no longer the object of his supreme love, nor the fountain of his pure delight, nor the blessed and only source of his bliss,—he rushed from his presence as from an object of terror, and sought concealment in Eden's bowers. That God whose presence was once so glorious, whose converse was so holy, whose voice was so sweet, became as a strange God to the rebellious and conscience-stricken creature, and, " absence from thee is best," was written in dark letters upon his guilty brow.

And whence this difference? Was God less glorious in himself? was he less holy, less loving, less faithful, or less the fountain of supreme bliss? Far from it. God has undergone no change. It is the perfection of a perfect Being that he is unchangeable; that he can never act contrary to his own nature, but must ever be, in all that he does, in harmony with himself. The change was in the creature. Adam had left his first love, had transferred his affections to another and an inferior object; and conscious that he had ceased to love God, he would fain have veiled himself from his presence, and have excluded himself from his communion. It is even so in the experience of a believer, conscious of declension in his love to God. There is a hiding from his presence; there are misty views of his character, misinterpretations of his dealings, and a lessening of holy desire for him: but where the heart is right in its affections, warm in its love, fixed in its desires, God is glorious in his perfections, and communion with him the highest bliss on earth. This was David's experience,— "O God, thou art my God; early will I seek thee: my soul thirsteth for thee, my flesh longeth for thee in a dry and thirsty land where no water is; to see thy power and thy glory, so as I have seen thee in the sanctuary. Because thy loving-kindness is better than life, my lips shall praise thee." Ps. lxiii. 1-3.

Not only in the declension of Divine love in the soul, does God become less an object of adoring contemplation and desire, but *there is less filial approach to Him*. The sweet confidence and simple trust of the child is lost; the soul no longer rushes into his bosom with all the lowly yet fond yearnings of an adopted son, but lingers at a distance; or, if it attempts to approach, does so with the trembling and the restraint of a slave. The tender, loving, child-like spirit, that marked the walk of the believer in the days of his espousals, when no object was so glorious to him as God, no being so loved as his heavenly Father, no spot so sacred as the throne of communion, no theme so sweet as his free grace adoption, has in a great degree departed; and distrust, and legal fears, and bondage of spirit, have succeeded it. All these sad effects may be traced to the declension of filial love in the soul of the believer towards God.

Hard thoughts of God in his dispensations, may be regarded as another undeniable symptom. The mark of a vigorous love to God is when the soul justifies God in all his wise and gracious dealings with it; rebels not, murmurs not, repines not, but meekly and silently acquiesces in the dispensation, be it never so trying. Divine love in the heart, deepening and expanding towards that God from whence it springs, will, in the hour of trial, exclaim, "My God has smitten me, but he is my

God still, faithful and loving. My father has chastened me sore, but he is my Father still, tender and kind. This trying dispensation originated in love, it speaks with the voice of love, it bears with it the message of love, and is sent to draw my heart closer and yet closer to the God of love, from whom it came." Dear reader, art thou one of the Lord's afflicted ones? Happy art thou if this is the holy and blessed result of his dealings with thee. Happy if thou heardest the voice of love in the rod, winning thy lone and sorrowful heart to the God from whom it came. But when love to God has declined, the reverse of this is the state of a tried and afflicted believer.

When there is but little inclination for communion with God, and the throne of grace is sought as a duty rather than a privilege, and, consequently, but little fellowship is experienced, a stronger evidence we need not of a declension of love in the soul. The more any object is to us a source of sweet delight and contemplation, the more strongly do we desire its presence, and the more restless are we in its absence. The friend we love we want constantly at our side; the spirit goes out in longings for communion with him,—his presence sweetens, his absence embitters, every other joy. Precisely true is this of God. He who knows God, who, with faith's eye, has discovered some of his glory, and by the power of the Spirit has felt something of his love, will not be at a loss to distinguish between God's sensible presence and absence in the soul. Some professing people walk so much without communion, without fellowship, without daily filial and close intercourse with God; they are so immersed in the cares, and so lost in the fogs and mists of the world; the fine edge of their spiritual affection is so blunted, and their love so frozen by contact with worldly influences and occupations,—and no less so, with cold, formal professors,—that the Sun of righteousness may cease to shine upon their soul, and they not know it! God may cease to visit them, and his absence not be felt! He may cease to speak, and the stillness of his voice not awaken an emotion of alarm! Yea, a more strange thing would happen to them, if the Lord were suddenly to break in upon their soul, with a visit of love, than were he to leave them for weeks and months without any token of his presence. Reader, art thou a professing child of God? Content not thyself to live thus; it is a poor, lifeless existence, unworthy of thy profession, unworthy of Him whose name thou dost bear, and unworthy of the glorious destiny towards which thou art looking. Thus may a believer test the character of his love: he, in whose heart Divine affection deepens, increases, and expands, finds God an object of increasing delight and desire, and communion with him the most costly privilege on earth: he cannot live in the neglect of constant, secret, and close fellowship with his God, his best and most faithful Friend.

When there is a less tender walk with God, we may be at no loss to ascertain the state of our love. What do we mean by a tender walk? When a believer walks in holy circumspection, in uprightness, integrity, close vigilance, and prayerfulness, before God, he then walks softly: "I shall go softly all my years." Isa. xxxviii. 15. When with filial tenderness, he trembles to offend his Father, his God, his best Friend,— when he increasingly delights himself in the precepts and commandments of the Lord,—when he would rather pluck from himself the right eye, and sever the right hand, than wilfully and knowingly offend God, and grieve the Spirit; *then* his walk is tender and soft and close with God. And what constrains a believer to this glorious life, this holy, hidden walk, but the love of God shed abroad in his heart? Imagine, then, what dangers must throng the path, what temptations must beset the soul, in whom the precious and influential grace of love is in a state of declension and decay!

Need we add, *when Christ is less glorious to the eye, and less precious to the heart*, Divine love in the soul of a believer must be on the wane? it cannot be otherwise. Our views of Jesus must be materially affected by the state of our affections towards him. When there is but little dealing with the atoning blood, leaning upon the righteousness, drawing from the fulness, and bearing daily the cross of Christ, the love of a believer waxeth cold. We would judge the depth of a man's Christianity, by his reply to the question, "'What think ye of Christ?' Is he lived to, is he lived upon? is his name your delight, his cross your boast, his work your resting place?" This will be your blessed experience, if the pulse of Divine love beats strong in your breast for Christ.

A decay of love to the saints of God, is a strong evidence of a decay of love to God himself. If we love God with a sincere and deepening affection, we must love his image wherever we find it. It is true, the picture may be but an imperfect copy, the outline may be but faintly drawn; there may be shades we cannot approve of; yet, recognising in the work the hand of the Spirit, and in the outline some resemblance to Him whom our souls admire and love, we must feel a drawing out of our holiest affections towards the object; we shall not pause before the surrender is made, to inquire to what section of the church of Christ he belongs, what name he bears, or what the colour of his uniform; but, discovering the man of God, the meek and lowly follower of Jesus, our heart and our hand are freely offered. O what a passport to our hearts is the image of Jesus in a child of God! Do we trace Christ in the principles that guide him, in the motives that govern him, in the spirit, in the very looks of the man? —we feel that we must take him to our bosom for Jesus' sake. O, it marks the decay of love to God in the soul, when the heart beats faintly, and the eye looks coldly, towards any dear saint of God, because he belongs not to our party, and wears not our badge; when bigotry, narrow-minded selfishness, warps the mind, congeals the current of love, and almost unchristianises a believer. The word of God is solemn and decisive on this point: "If a man say, I love God, and hateth his brother, he is a liar; for he that loveth not his brother whom he hath seen, how can he love God whom he hath not seen? And this commandment have we from him, that he who loveth God, love his brother also." 1 John iv. 20, 21. "By this," says Jesus, "shall all men know that ye are my disciples, if ye love one another." If we love not the visible resemblance, how can we love the invisible Archetype?

When love to God declines, with it will decline *an interest in the advancement and prosperity of his cause*: the one invariably follows the other. We do not say that outward zeal may not continue long after a process of concealed declension has advanced in the soul, and secret duties have become neglected—this is the lamentable case with many; but a true, spiritual, and lively interest in the increase of Christ's kingdom, in the diffusion of his truth, the deepening of holiness in the church, the conversion of sinners, will invariably decline with the declension of love to God. And when we mark a member of a church maintaining his external union, and yet hanging as a dead and fruitless branch upon the vine, doing nothing to advance the cause of God and truth, withholding his money, his prayers, his personal attendance on the means of grace, and rather opposing than cheering on the active portion of the body, we are ready to ask, "How dwelleth the love of God in him?"

The declension of love may be traced to many CAUSES: we can enumerate but a few; let the following be seriously pondered. *Worldly encroachment* is a fruitful cause; no two affections can be more opposite and antagonistic than love to God and love to the world: it is impossible that they can both exist with equal force in the same breast; the one or the other must be supreme,—they cannot occupy the same throne. If a Divine affection is regent, then the world is excluded; but if an earthly affection, a grovelling and increasing love to the world governs—God is shut out: the one must give place to the other. Love to God will expel love to the world; love to the world will deaden the soul's love to God. "No man can serve two masters": it is impossible to love God *and* the world, to serve him *and* mammon. Here is a most fertile cause of declension in Divine love; guard against it as you would fortify yourself against your greatest foe. It is a vortex that has engulfed millions of souls; multitudes of professing Christians have been drawn into its eddy, and have gone down into its gulf. This enemy of your soul will steal upon you by silent and insidious encroachment. It has its disguises many. It will present itself masked in a proper regard for business, in a diligence in lawful callings, a prudent yielding to domestic claims, and will even quote scriptural precept and example, and assume the form of an angel of light; but suspect it, guard against it. Remember what is recorded by the apostle of a primitive professor: "Demas hath forsaken me, *having loved this present world*." Be not a modern Demas: "Love not the world, neither the things that are in the world; if any man love the world, the love of the Father is not in him." No Christian man can maintain his spirituality unimpaired, his love uninjured, his robe unspotted, his walk irreproachable, who secretly admits the world to his heart. How can he exemplify the life of a pilgrim and a sojourner; how can his heart rise in a constant flame of love to God? What attraction can the throne of grace have, what zest in spiritual duties, what delight in the communion of saints, while his heart goes out after covetousness, and worldly ambition, love of place, and human applause are the rival passions of his soul? Let it, then, be solemnly remembered, that an inordinate, uncrucified attachment to the world, must be parted with, if the precious grace of love to God is to enthrone itself in the affections of the believer.

An idolatrous and unsanctified attachment to the creature, has again and again crucified love to Christ in the heart. Upon the same principle that no man can love the world and God

with a like supreme and kindred affection, so no man can give
to Christ and the creature the same intensity of regard. And
yet, how often has the creature stolen the heart from its lawful Sovereign! That heart that was once so simply and so
supremely the Lord's,—those affections that clung to him with
such purity and power of grasp, have now been transferred
to another and inferior object: the piece of clay that God had
given but to deepen the obligation and heighten the soul's
love to himself, has been moulded into an idol, before which
the heart pours its daily incense; the flower that he has caused
to spring forth, but to endear his own beauty and make his
own name more fragrant, has supplanted the "Rose of
Sharon" in the bosom. Oh! is it *thus* that we abuse our
mercies? is it thus that we convert our blessings into poisons?
that we allow the things that were sent to endear the heart of
our God, and to make the cross, through which they came,
more precious, to allure our affections from their holy and
blessed centre? Fools that we are, to love the creature more
than the Creator! Dear reader, why has God been disciplining thee as, it may be, he has? why has he removed thine
idols, crumbled into dust thy piece of clay, and blown wither-
ingly upon thy beauteous flower?—why? because he hateth
idolatry; and idolatry is essentially the same, whether it be
offered to a lifeless, shapeless stock, or to a spirit of intellect
and beauty. And what speaks his voice in every stream that
he dries, in every plant that he blows upon, and in every disappointment he writes upon the creature?—"My son, give
me thine heart. I want thy love, thy pure and supreme affection; I want to be the one and only object of thy delight. I
gave my Son for thee—his life for thine; I sent my Spirit to
quicken, to renew, to seal, and to possess thee for myself: all
this I did, that I might have thine heart. To possess myself
of this, I have smitten thy gourds, removed thine idols, broken
thine earthly dependences, and have sought to detach thy
affections from the creature, that they may rise, undivided

and unfettered, and entwine around one who loves thee with an undying love."

Again; *interpreting God's covenant dealings in the light of judgments rather than the fruits of love,* will tend greatly to deaden the soul's affections towards God. Hard and harsh thoughts of God will be the effect of wrong interpretations of his dealings: if for one moment we remove the eye from off the heart of God in the hour and depth of our trial, we are prepared to give heed to every dark suggestion of the adversary; that moment we look at the dispensation with a different mind, and to God with an altered affection; we view the chastisement as the effect of displeasure, and the covenant God that sent it, as unkind, unloving, and severe. But let faith's eagle-eye pierce the clouds and darkness that surround the throne, and behold the *heart* of God is still *love,* all love, and nothing but love, to his afflicted, bereaved, and sorrow-stricken child, and in a moment every murmur will be hushed, every rebellious feeling will be still, and every unkind thought will lay in the dust; and, " He hath done all things well,—in love and faithfulness hath he afflicted me," will be the only sounds uttered by the lips. If, then, beloved, you would have your heart always fixed on God, its affections flowing in one unbroken current towards him, interpret every dispensation that he sends in the light of his *love;* never suffer yourself to be betrayed into the belief, that any other feeling prompts the discipline; give not place to the suggestion for one moment,— banish it from the threshold of your mind, the moment it seeks an entrance. And let this be the reflection that hushes and soothes you to repose, even as an infant upon its mother's breast: " My God is love! my Father is unchangeable tenderness and truth! he hath done it, and it is well done."

Let us now turn to the consideration of the *revival* of this waning grace in the child of God; but before any especial means of revival are suggested or adopted, *let the believer seek to know the exact state of his love to God.* A knowledge of

himself, is the first step in the return of every soul to God. In
conversion, it was self-knowledge—a knowledge of ourselves
as utterly lost—that led us to Jesus; thus did the Eternal Spirit
teach, and thus he led us to the great and finished work of the
Son of God. Before, then, you fall upon any means of revival, ascertain the exact state of your love, and what has
caused its declension; shrink not from the examination,—turn
not from the discovery. And should the humiliating truth
force itself upon you,—" I am not as I once was; my soul has
lost ground,—my spirituality of mind has decayed;—I have
lost the fervour of my first love—have slackened in the heavenly race; Jesus is not as he once was, the joy of my day, the
song of my night;—and my walk with God is no longer so
tender, loving, and filial as it was,"—then honestly and
humbly confess it before God. To be humbled as we should
be, we must know ourselves; there must be no disguising of
our true condition from ourselves, nor from God; there must
be no framing of excuses for our declensions: the wound
must be probed, the disease must be known, and its most
aggravated symptoms brought to view. Ascertain, then, the
true state of your affection towards God; bring your love to
him, to the touchstone of truth; see how far it has declined,
and thus you will be prepared for the second step in the work
of revival, which is, to—

Trace out and crucify the cause of your declension in love.
Where love declines, there must be a cause; and when ascer-
tained, it must be immediately removed. Love to God is a
tender flower; it is a sensitive plant, soon and easily crushed;
perpetual vigilance is needed to preserve it in a healthy, growing state. The world's heat will wither it, the coldness of
formal profession will often nip it: a thousand influences, all
foreign to its nature and hostile to its growth, are leagued
against it; the soil in which it is placed is not genial to it. " In
the flesh there dwelleth no good thing "; whatever of holiness
is in the believer, whatever breathing after Divine conformity,

whatever soaring of the affections towards God, is from God himself, and is there as the result of sovereign grace. "That which is born of the flesh is flesh; and that which is born of the Spirit is spirit." What sleepless vigilance, then, and what perpetual culture are needed, to preserve the bloom and the fragrance, and to nourish the growth of this celestial plant! Search out and remove the cause of the declension and decay of this precious grace of the Spirit; rest not until it is discovered and brought to light. Should it prove to be the *world*, come out from it, and be ye separate, and touch not the unclean thing; or the power of *indwelling sin*, seek its immediate crucifixion by the cross of Jesus. Does the *creature* steal thy heart from Christ, and deaden thy love to God?—resign it at God's bidding; he asks the surrender of thine heart, and has promised to be better to thee than all creature love. All the tenderness, the fond affection, the acute sympathy, the true fidelity, that thou ever didst find or enjoy in the creature, dwells in God, thy covenant God and Father, in an infinite degree. He makes the creature all it is to thee: that fond smile which thy fellow-believer beamed upon thee, was but a ray from his countenance; that expression of love was but a drop from his heart; that tenderness and sympathy was a part of his nature. Then, possessing God in Christ, you can desire no more,—you can have no more: if he asks the surrender of the creature, cheerfully resign it; and let God be all in all to thee. This suggests a second direction:—

Draw largely from the fount of love in God. All love to God in the soul is the result of his love to us; it is begotten in the heart by his Spirit,—" We love him, because he first loved us " : he took the first step, and made the first advance,—" He *first* loved us." O heart-melting truth! The love of God to us when yet we were sinners, who can unfold it? what mortal tongue can describe it? Before we had any being, and when we were enemies, he sent his Son to die for us; and when we were far off by wicked works, he sent his Spirit to bring us to him in the cloudy and dark day. All his dealings with us since then—his patience, restoring mercies, tender, loving, faithful care, yea, the very strokes of his rod, have but unfolded the depths of his love towards his people: this is the love we desire you to be filled with. "The Lord direct your hearts into the love of God." Draw largely from this river; why should you deny yourselves? There is enough love in God to overflow the hearts of all his saints through all eternity; then why not be filled? "The Lord direct your hearts *into* the love of God"; stand not upon the brink of the fountain, linger not upon the margin of this river,—enter *into* it— plunge *into* it; it is for thee,—poor, worthless, unworthy, vile as thou feelest thyself to be,—this river of love is yet for *thee*! Seek to be filled with it, that ye may know the love of Christ which passeth knowledge, and that your heart in return may ascend in a flame of love to God.

Deal much and closely with a crucified Saviour. Here is the grand secret of a constant ascending of the affections to God. If thou dost find it difficult to comprehend the love of God towards thee, read it in the cross of his dear Son. "In this was manifested the love of God towards us, because that God sent his only-begotten Son into the world, that we might live through him. Herein is love, not that we loved God, but that he loved us, and sent his Son to be the propitiation for our sins." 1 John iv. 9, 10. Dwell upon this amazing fact; drink into this precious truth; muse upon it, ponder it, search into it, pray over it, until your heart is melted down, and broken, and overwhelmed with God's wondrous love to you, in the gift of Jesus. O how will this rekindle the flame that is ready to die in your bosom! how it will draw you up in a holy and unreserved surrender of body, soul, and spirit! Forget not, then, to deal much with Jesus. Whenever thou detectest a waning of love, a reluctance to take up the daily cross, a shrinking from the precept, go immediately to Calvary; go simply and directly to Jesus; get thy heart warmed with ardent love by contemplating him upon the cross, and soon will the frosts that gather round it melt away, the congealed current shall begin to flow, and the " chariots of Amminadib " shall bear thy soul away to communion and fellowship with God.

Do not fail to honour the Holy Spirit in this great work of revival. The work is all his; beware of taking it out of his hands. The means we have suggested for the revival of this waning grace of love, can only be rendered effectual as the Spirit worketh in you, and worketh with you. Pray much for his anointings; go to him as the Glorifier of Christ, as the Comforter, the Sealer, the Witness, the Earnest of his people : it is he that will apply the atoning blood,—it is he that will revive thy drooping graces,—it is he that will fan to a flame thy waning love, by unfolding the cross, and directing your heart into the love of God. Take not your eye off the love of the Spirit; his love is equal with the Father's and the Son's love. Honour him in his love, let it encourage thee to draw largely from his influences, and to be " filled with the Spirit."

Lastly : *remember that though your love has waxed cold, the love of thy God and Father towards thee has undergone no diminution:* not the shadow of a change has it known. Although he has hated thy declension, has rebuked thy wandering, yet his *love* he has not withdrawn from thee. What an encouragement to return to him again! Not one moment has God turned his back upon thee, though thou hast turned thy back upon him times without number : his face has always been towards thee; and it would have shone upon thee with all its melting power, but for the clouds which thine own waywardness and sinfulness have caused to obscure and hide from thee its blessed light. Retrace thy steps and return again to God. Though thou hast been a poor wanderer and hast left thy first love,—though thy affections have strayed from the Lord, and thy heart has gone after other lovers, still God is gracious and ready to pardon; he will welcome thee back again for the sake of Jesus, his beloved Son in whom he is well pleased, for this is his own blessed declaration,—" If his children forsake my law, and walk not in my judgments; if they break my statutes, and keep not my commandments; then will I visit their transgressions with a rod, and their iniquity with stripes. Nevertheless, my loving-kindness will I not utterly take from him, nor suffer my faithfulness to fail." Psalm lxxxix. 30-33.

CHAPTER III

DECLENSION IN FAITH

" Lord, increase our faith."—Luke xvii. 5.

EACH grace of the Spirit must be considered by the believer as forming an essential element of his Christian character, and, as such, inconceivably costly and precious. He may not be sensible of possessing them all in the same degree: for as we only know the extent of our mental or physical powers, as circumstances develop them, so a believer knows not what graces of the Spirit he may possess, until the dealings of a covenant God call them into holy and active exercise. Thus do infinite wisdom and goodness unfold themselves in all the transactions of God with his people. Not arbitrarily, nor wantonly, nor unnecessarily does the heavenly Father deal with his child;—every stroke of the rod is but the muffled voice of love; every billow bears on its bosom, and every tempest on its wing, some new and rich blessing from the better land. O that we should ever breathe a sigh, or utter a murmur at God's covenant dealings, or for one moment mistake their holy and wise design and tendency!

If, then, every grace of the Spirit be thus indispensable and costly, the declension and decay of that grace in the believer must attract the especial notice of God, and involve solemn and serious consequences. Any part of God's great and gracious work of grace in the soul that is suffered to decay, seems like a reflection upon God himself; there is a dishonouring of him in it to a degree of which the believer is but little aware. What, next to his Son, is most glorious, and costly, and precious in God's sight? Is it the world?—nay, he sees no glory in that. Is it the heavens?—nay, they are not clean in his sight, and he chargeth his angels with folly: what is it, then? —it is his kingdom in his saints, his renewing, adopting, sanctifying grace in his people. Next to his Son, nothing is so glorious and costly; he sees, compared with this, no real beauty in aught besides; here his profoundest thoughts dwell, here his fondest love rests; to commence, carry forward and perfect this, all his arrangements in the vast provinces of nature, providence, and grace, are rendered subservient. Let us imagine, then, what must be the mind of God in view of a decaying, declining state of grace in the soul, and what the peculiar method which he adopts to resuscitate and recover it. Having considered personal declension in two of its stages, we have arrived at another equally solemn and important,— the declension of the grace of faith. We shall adopt the same plan in discussing it; and proceed, in the outset, to unfold the scriptural nature and properties of this Christian grace.

Few subjects within the vast range of Christian theology have been more frequently discussed, and yet, perhaps, so little understood, as that of faith. Nor is it to be wondered at, that men who approach its investigation without strict regard to the simple teaching of God's word, and entire dependence upon the illumination of the Spirit, should find difficulty and even obscurity investing a subject so purely spiritual. Nor is Satan slothful in his attempts to obscure the minds of men in their researches into this great subject. Faith is that grace against which the attacks of Satan are more directly and constantly directed than almost any other. Not ignorant of its spiritual nature and essential importance; and knowing the great glory its exercise brings to God, the subtle and sleepless foe of the believer employs every art to mystify its simplicity, and neutralise its efforts. It is not surprising, then, that opinions upon a subject so important should often be conflicting, and that views of its nature should often be obscure.

And yet scriptural and spiritual views of faith form the very basis of experimental godliness. Faith, being the starting point of experimental religion, an error here must prove fatal to every succeeding step. It is of no real moment how beautiful that religious structure is, or how perfect its symmetry, and magnificent its archings, and lofty its turrets, if it is based upon an *unsound faith*. No system of religion, no doctrinal creed, no profession of Christianity, if it cannot bear the test of God's word, and is not found to answer that test, is of any real value. All mere religion of the intellect, and of the imagination, and of taste—and these only are popular with the world—resting upon an unscriptural and defective faith, are but splendid chimeras; they disappoint in periods of sorrow, they deceive in the hour of death, and they involve the soul in interminable woe in the world to come. It is, then, of the most solemn moment, that, in professing religion, a man should see that he starts with *true faith*. If a merchant, in balancing his books, commences with an error in his calculations, is it surprising that that error should extend throughout his account, and bring him to a wrong conclusion? Or, if a traveller, journeying towards his home, selects from the many roads that branch out before him, a wrong one, would it be any marvel if he should never arrive at it? Apply these simple illustrations to the subject before us. Man has a long and a solemn account to settle with God; he is a debtor to a large amount; he owes God a perfect obedience to his law, and has " nothing to pay." Yet another character: he is a traveller to eternity, and every step is conducting him towards the close of a brief but responsible probation. Now, if in his religion he commences with unsound, unwarrantable, unscriptural views of any *essential doctrine of salvation*, the error with which he commenced must affect his entire religion; and unless his steps are retraced, and the error discovered and corrected, the end must prove fatal to his eternal happiness. He who pens this page feels it of the most solemn importance, that this chapter should present a scriptural view of the nature, properties, and tendency of this essential part of the great plan of salvation. May the Spirit now be our teacher, and the word of God our text-book!

It may be proper to state, that the authors of systems of divinity have generally classified the subject of faith. They speak of speculative faith,—of historical faith,—practical faith,—saving faith,—realizing faith. But as these distinctions serve only to mystify the subject and perplex the mind, and frequently lead to great errors, we set them aside, preferring and adopting the simple nomenclature of the inspired word, which can never perplex or mislead the humble disciple of Jesus.

The Holy Ghost speaks of but " one faith," Eph. iv. 5, and that faith the " faith of God's elect." Tit. i. 1. And still the question recurs, What is faith? Briefly and simply, it is that act of the understanding and the heart by which a repenting sinner—a sinner under the mighty operation of the Eternal Spirit, convincing him of sin, and working in him true contrition—closes in with God's free proclamation of pardon through a crucified Saviour : he believes, he receives, he welcomes the promise of eternal life through the Lord Jesus Christ, and thus " sets to his seal that God is true." We speak of the *understanding* as included in this act, because the advocates of evangelical truth have been accused of advancing doctrines which render nugatory all mental operation, and which make religion to consist in mere *feeling*. This witness is not true. We maintain that every faculty of the human mind is brought out in its full power, in the great work of heart-religion; that the Holy Spirit, working repentance and faith in a man, does more to develop the intellectual faculties, than all human teaching beside. Have we not seen individuals, who, before conversion, gave no evidence of any than the most ordinary powers of mind, become, through the illumination of the Spirit by the revealed word, strong and commanding in intellect! Powers of reasoning, hitherto hidden, were developed; and fountains of thought, hitherto sealed up, were opened; old things passed away, and all things became new. We repeat, then, it is the tendency of true religion to develop and strengthen the human intellect, and to give intensity and acuteness to all its faculties. No mind is so powerful as a *renewed* and *sanctified* mind.

Faith, then, has to do with the *understanding* and the *heart*. A man must *know* his lost and ruined condition before he will accept of Christ; and how can he know this, without a spiritually-enlightened mind? What a surprising change now passes over the man! He is brought, by the mighty power of the Holy Ghost, to a knowledge of himself; one beam of light, one touch of the Spirit, has altered all his views of himself, has placed him in a new aspect; all his thoughts, his affections, his desires, are diverted into another and an opposite channel; his fond views of his own righteousness have fled like a dream; his high thoughts are humbled, his lofty looks are brought low, and, as a broken-hearted sinner, he takes his place in the dust before God. O wondrous, O blessed change! to see the Pharisee take the place, and to hear him utter the cry, of the Publican,—" God be merciful to me a sinner!"— to hear him exclaim, " I am lost, self-ruined, deserving eternal wrath; and of sinners, the vilest and the chief!" And now the work and exercise of faith commences; the same blessed Spirit that convinced of sin, presents to the soul a Saviour crucified for the lost,—unfolds a salvation full and free for the most worthless,—reveals a fountain that " cleanses from all sin," and holds up to view a righteousness that " justifies from all things." And all that he sets the poor convinced sinner upon doing to avail himself of this, is simply to *believe*. To the momentous question, "What shall I do to be saved?" this is the only reply,—" Believe in the Lord Jesus Christ, and thou shalt be saved." The anxious soul eagerly exclaims,—" Have I then nothing to do but to *believe?*—have I no great work to accomplish?—no price to bring, no worthiness to plead?—may I come just as I am, without merit, without self-preparation, without money, with all my vileness and nothingness?" Still the reply is, " Only believe ": " Then, Lord, I *do* believe," exclaims the soul in a transport of joy, " help thou my unbelief!" This, reader, is *faith*; faith, that wondrous grace, that mighty act of which you have heard so much, upon which so many volumes have been written, and so many sermons have been preached; it is the simple rolling of a wounded, bleeding heart, upon a wounded, bleeding Saviour; it is the simple reception of the amazing truth, that Jesus died for the *ungodly* —died for *sinners*—died for the *poor*, the *vile*, the *bankrupt*; that he invites and welcomes to his bosom all poor, convinced, heavy-laden *sinners*. The heart, believing this wondrous announcement, going out of all other dependences and resting only in this,—receiving it, welcoming it, rejoicing in it, in a moment, all, all is peace. Forget not, then, reader, the simple definition of faith,—it is but to believe with all the heart *that Jesus died for sinners*; and the full belief of this one fact will bring peace to the most anxious and sin-troubled soul.

" Having begun in the Spirit," the believer is not to be "made perfect in the flesh"; having commenced his Divine life in faith, in faith he is to walk every step of his journey homewards. The entire spiritual life of a child of God is a life of faith,—God has so ordained it: and to bring him into the full and blessed experience of it, is the end of all his parental dealings with him. The moment a poor sinner has touched the hem of Christ's garment, feeble though this act of faith be, it is yet the commencement of this high and holy life; even from that moment, the believing soul professes to have done with a life of sense—with second causes, and to have entered

upon a glorious life of faith on Christ. It is no forced application to him of the apostle's declaration: " I am crucified
with Christ; nevertheless I live, yet not I, but Christ liveth in
me; and the life which I *now* live in the flesh, I live by the
faith of the Son of God." Let us briefly unfold some peculiar
points of blessedness in this life.

There is its *security*: a believer *stands* by faith,—"Thou
standest by faith." Rom. xi. 20. Why is it that thou hast
been kept to the present moment? Thou hast seen many a tall
cedar bowed to the earth; many who did appear to " run
well," but who, in the hour of temptation, when worldly
power, and wealth, and distinction increased, made shipwreck
of their fancied faith, and fell into divers lusts and snares
which drowned their souls. Why hast *thou* been kept? thy
vessel weathering the storm, thy feet yet upon the rock? Because " thou standest by faith,"—the " faith of God's elect "
has kept thee; and though thou art deeply conscious of many
and great departures,—sins, it may be, which if known to an
ungodly, ignorant world, would bring upon thee the laugh of
scorn,—yet thou hast never been left quite to unhinge thy
soul from Jesus; thou hast discovered thy sins, and mourned
over and confessed them, and sought their forgiveness through
a fresh application of the atoning blood,—and still, " thou
standest by faith." Ah! if faith had not kept thee, where
wouldst thou *now* have been? where would that temptation have driven thee? into what consequences would that
sin have involved thee? But O, that brokenness, that
contrition, that mourning, that going afresh to the open
fountain, doth prove that there was that in thee which
would not let thee *quite depart*! The cedar may have been
bowed to the earth, but it has risen again; the vessel may
have been tossed in the tempest, and even may have been
worsted by the storm, yet it hath found its port: the " faith
of God's elect " has kept thee. " Be not high-minded, but
fear." Thine own vigilance, and power, and wisdom, had

been but poor safeguards, but for the indwelling of that faith that can never die.

There is, too, the *peculiar blessedness* of the life of faith: "We walk by faith, not by sight." 2 Cor. v. 7. This walk of faith takes in all the minute circumstances of every day's history; a walking *every step* by faith: a looking above trials, above necessities, above perplexities, above improbabilities and impossibilities, above all second causes; and, in the face of difficulties and discouragements, going forward, leaning upon God. If the Lord were to roll the Red Sea before us, and marshal the Egyptians behind us, and thus, hemming us in on every side, should yet bid us *advance*, it would be the duty and the privilege of faith instantly to obey,—believing, that, ere our feet touched the water, God, in our extremity, would divide the sea, and take us dry-shod over it. This is the only holy and happy life of a believer; if he for a moment leaves this path, and attempts to walk *by sight*, difficulties will throng around him, troubles will multiply, the smallest trials will become heavy crosses, temptations to depart from the simple and upright walk will increase in number and power, the heart will sicken at disappointment, the Spirit will be grieved, and God will be dishonoured. Let this precious truth ever be before the mind,—"We walk by faith, not by sight."

Faith is an essential part of the spiritual armour: "Above all, taking *the shield of faith*, wherewith ye shall be able to quench the fiery darts of the wicked." Eph. vi. 16. Faith is also spoken of as the believer's breast-plate: "But let us, who are of the day, be sober, putting on *the breast-plate of faith*." 1 Thess. v. 8. There is not a moment, even the holiest, but we are exposed to the "fiery darts" of the adversary. The onset, too, is often at a moment when we least suspect its approach; seasons of peculiar nearness to God, of hallowed enjoyment,—"for we wrestle not against flesh and blood, but against principalities, against powers, against the rulers of the darkness of this world, against spiritual wickedness in high places" (*marg.* " heavenly places "),—are frequently selected as the occasion of attack. But, clad in this armour,—the shield and the breast-plate of faith,—no weapon formed against us shall prosper; the " fiery dart " shall be quenched, and the enemy shall be put to flight. Faith in a crucified, risen, conquering, exalted Saviour,—faith in a present and ever-living Head,—faith eyeing future glory, the crown glittering, and the palm waving in its view, is the faith that overcomes and triumphs. Faith dealing constantly and simply with Jesus,—flying to his atoning blood, drawing from his fulness, and at all times and under all circumstances looking unto him, will ever bring a conflicting soul off more than conqueror : " This is the *victory* that overcometh the world, even our faith. Who is he that overcometh the world, but he that be-lieveth that Jesus is the Son of God?"

Faith is a purifying grace: " Purifying their hearts by faith," Acts xv. 9; " Sanctified by faith that is in me," xxvi. 18. It is a principle holy in its nature and tendency; he is most holy who has most faith; he who has least faith is most exposed to the assaults of his inbred corruptions. If there is in any child of God a desire for Divine conformity, for more of the spirit of Christ, more weanedness, and crucifixion, and daily dying, this should be his ceaseless prayer,—" Lord, increase my faith." Faith in Jesus checks the power of sin, slays the hidden corruption, and enables the believer to " endure as seeing him who is invisible."

This, too, is the grace that smooths the rugged way, lightens the daily burthen, " glorifies God in the fire "; is " the sub-stance of things hoped for, the evidence of things not seen "; rests upon God's word because he has said it; and keeps the soul, through all its conflicts and trials, safe unto eternal glory : " Kept by the power of God, *through faith*, unto sal-vation." But we have mainly to do with the *declension* of this precious grace.

We have already remarked, that there is nothing essentially omnipotent in any single grace of the Spirit; to suppose this, would be to deify that grace : that, although regeneration is a spiritual work, and all the graces implanted in the soul are the product of the Spirit, and must necessarily be in their nature spiritual and indestructible, yet they may so *decline* in their power, become so enfeebled and impaired in their vigour and tendency, as to be classed among the " things that are ready to die." It is pre-eminently so with faith; perhaps there is no part of the Spirit's work more constantly and severely assailed, and consequently more exposed to declension, than this. Shall we look at the *examples* in God's word? We cite the case of *Abraham*, the father of the faithful; beholding him, at God's command, binding his son upon the altar, and raising the knife for the sacrifice, we unhesitatingly exclaim,— " Surely never was faith like this! Here is faith of a giant character; faith, whose sinews no trial can ever relax, whose lustre no temptation can ever dim." And yet, tracing the history of the patriarch still further, we find that very giant faith now trembling, and yielding under a trial far less acute and severe; he, who could surrender the life of his promised son—that son, through whose lineal descent Jesus was to come—into the hands of God, could not entrust that same God with his own. We look at *Job* : in the commencement of his deep trial we find him justifying God; messenger follows messenger with tidings of yet deeper woe, but not a murmur is breathed; and as the cup, now full to the brim, is placed to his lips, how sweetly sounds the voice of holy resignation,—" The Lord gave, and the Lord hath taken away; blessed be the name of the Lord "; " In all this did not Job sin with his lips " : and yet the very faith, which thus bowed in meekness to the rod, so *declined*, as to lead him to curse the day of his birth! We see *David*, whose faith could at one time lead him out to battle with Goliath, now fleeing from a shadow, and exclaiming,—" I shall one day perish by the hand of Saul!" And mark how the energy of *Peter's* faith declined, who at one period could walk boldly upon the tempestuous sea, and yet at another could deny his Lord, panic-struck at the voice of a little maid. Who will say that the faith of the holiest man of God may not at one time greatly and sadly decline?

But we need not travel *out of ourselves* for the evidence and the illustration of the affecting truth we are upon: let every believer turn in upon himself. What, reader, is the real state of your faith? is it as lively, vigorous, and active, as it was when you first believed? Has it undergone no declension? Is the Object of faith as glorious in your eye as he then was? Are you not now looking at second causes in God's dealings with you, instead of lifting thine eye and fixing it on him alone? What is your faith in prayer?—do you come boldly to the throne of grace, asking, nothing doubting? Do you take all your trials, your wants, your infirmities, to God! What is your realisation of eternal things,—is faith here in constant, holy exercise? Art thou living as a pilgrim and a sojourner, " choosing rather to suffer affliction with the people of God," than float along on the summer-sea of this world's enjoyments? What is the crucifying power of your faith?— does it deaden you to sin, and wean you from the world, and constrain you to walk humbly with God and near to Jesus? And when the Lord brings the cross, and says, " Bear this for me," does your faith promptly and cheerfully acquiesce, " any cross, any suffering, any sacrifice for thee, dear Lord?" Thus may you try the nature and the degree of your faith; bring it to the touchstone of God's truth, and ascertain what its character is, and how far it has suffered declension. Permit us to adduce a few *causes* to which a feeble and declining faith may frequently be traced.

When a believer's visits to his closet grow less frequent and spiritual, faith will assuredly decline. Prayer is the channel that supplies faith with its nourishment and vigour. As well might we cut off all the rills and streams which flow down the mountain's side, and expect that the valleys beneath will present their enamelled and verdant aspect, as to close up the channel of prayer, and then look for a healthy, vigorous, and growing faith. There is a beautiful connexion between faith and prayer,—their influence is reciprocal: constant and ardent prayer strengthens faith, and faith, brought into exercise, stimulates to prayer. A praying man will be a believing man, and a man of faith will be a man of prayer. Mary Queen of Scotland is said to have expressed a greater dread of the prayers of John Knox the Reformer, than of all the armies leagued against her. But what infused such power into the prayers of Knox, rendering them " terrible as an army with banners?"—it was his mighty faith; and his mighty faith rendered him mighty in prayer. Here, then, we have one cause, and a most fruitful one, of the weak and powerless faith of many professors: they live at a *distance from God*, and the consequence is, faith receives no nourishment; there is but little going to Jesus, but little dealing with his blood, but little drawing from his fulness; forgetting that, as he is the Author, so is he the Sustainer of faith, and that the soul only lives, as it lives " by the faith of the Son of God." Reader, is thy faith in a feeble, sickly, declining state? Look well to thy closet: see if thou canst not trace the cause *there*. What is thy accustomed habit of prayer? How much time of twelve hours is spent with God? What! do thy business, thy family, thy worldly engagements, consume all thy time? What! but little time for prayer?—but few stolen moments for God? —no hours redeemed from secular pursuits, and devoted to holy communion and filial fellowship with thy Father in secret? Is it well nigh *all* consumed upon thyself, in worldly care, confusion, and excitement? Wonder not that thy faith is feeble, drooping, and ready to die: the greatest wonder is, that thou art not quite dead; that the feeble, flickering spark is not entirely extinguished. Rouse thee from thy fearful slumber! Thy situation, drowsy professor, is perilous in the extreme; thou art sleeping on enchanted ground; thy shield and thy breast-plate lying unbuckled at thy side, and all thine enemies gathering in fearful numbers around thee!—a return to prayer is thine only safety.

Dealing much with a life of sense, is a most influential cause of declension in faith. If we desire to *see* our way every step of our homeward path, we must abandon the more difficult, though more blessed ascent of faith; it is impossible to walk by sight and by faith at the same time; the two paths run in opposite directions. If the Lord were to reveal the *why* and the *wherefore* of all his dealings; if we were only to advance as we saw the spot on which we were to place our foot, or only to go out as we knew the place whither we were going, it then were no longer a life of faith that we lived, but of sight. We should have exchanged the life which *glorifies*, for the life which *dishonours* God. When God, about to deliver the Israelites from the power of Pharaoh, commanded them to *advance*, it was before he revealed the way by which he was about to rescue them. The Red Sea rolled its deep and frowning waves at their feet; they saw not a spot of dry ground on which they could tread; and yet, this was the command to Moses,—" Speak unto the children of Israel that they *go forward*." They were to " walk by faith, not by sight." It had been no exercise of faith in God, no confidence in his promise, no resting in his faithfulness, and no " magnifying of his word above all his name," had they halted until the waters clave asunder, and a dry passage opened to their view. But like the patriarchs, they " staggered not at the promise, of God through unbelief; but were strong in faith, giving glory to God." Have little to do *with sense*, if thou wouldst have much to do *with faith*. Expect not always to *see* the way. God may call you to go out into a place, not making known to you whither you go; but it is your duty, like Abraham, to obey. All that you ever have to do is to go forward, leaving all consequences and results to God: it is enough for you that the Lord by this providence says, "Go forward!" This is all you may hear; it is your duty instantly to respond, "Lord, I go at thy bidding; bid me come to thee, though it be upon the stormy water."

Faith unexercised in dark and afflictive providences, leads greatly to its declension. The exercise of faith strengthens, as the neglect to exercise weakens it. It is the constant play of the arm that brings out its muscular power in all its fulness; were that arm allowed to hang by our side, still and motionless, how soon would its sinews contract, and its energy waste away! So it is with faith, the right arm of a believer's strength; the more it is exercised, the mightier it becomes; neglect to use it, allow it to remain inert and inoperative, and the effect will be a withering up of its power. Now when gloomy providences, and sharp trials and temptations, thicken around a poor believing soul, *then* is it the time for faith to put on its strength, and come forth to the battle. God never places his child in any difficulties, or throws upon him any cross, but it is a call to exercise faith; and if the opportunity of its exercise passes away without improvement, the effect will be, a weakening of the principle, and a feeble putting forth of its power in the succeeding trial. Forget not, that the more faith is brought into play, the more it increases; the more it is exercised, the stronger it becomes; the reverse of this is frequently the cause of its sad declension.

The habitual, or even the occasional, doubtful apprehension indulged in of his interest in Christ, will tend materially to the enfeebling and decay of a believer's faith: no cause can be more certain in its effects than this. If it be true, as we have shown, that the exercise of faith develops its strength, it is equally true, that the perpetual indulgence of doubtful apprehensions of pardon and acceptance, must necessarily eat as a cankerworm at the root of faith. Every misgiving felt, every doubt cherished, every fear yielded to, every dark providence brooded over, tends to unhinge the soul from God, and dims its near and loving view of Jesus. To doubt the love, the wisdom, and the faithfulness of God; to doubt the perfection of the work of Christ; to doubt the operation of the Spirit on the heart,—what can tend more to the weakening and decay of this precious and costly grace? Every time the soul sinks under the pressure of a doubt of its interest in Christ, the effect must be a weakening of the soul's view of the glory, perfection, and all-sufficiency of Christ's work. But imperfectly may the doubting Christian be aware what dishonour is done to Jesus, what reflection is cast upon his great work, by every unbelieving fear he cherishes. It is a secret wounding of Jesus, however the soul may shrink from such an inference; it is a lowering, an undervaluing of Christ's obedience and death,—that glorious work of salvation with which the Father has declared himself well pleased,—that work with which Divine justice has confessed itself satisfied,—that work on the basis of which every poor, convinced sinner is saved, and on the ground of which millions of redeemed and glorified spirits are now bowing around the throne,—that work, we say, is dishonoured, undervalued, and slighted by every doubt and fear secretly harboured, or openly expressed by a child of God. The moment a believer looks at his unworthiness more than at the righteousness of Christ,—supposes that there is not a sufficiency of merit in Jesus to supply the absence of all merit in himself before God, what is it but a setting up his sinfulness and unworthiness *above* the infinite worth, fulness, and sufficiency of Christ's atonement and righteousness? There is much spurious humility among many of the dear saints of God. It is thought by some, that to be always doubting one's pardon and acceptance, is the evidence of a lowly spirit. It is, allow us to say, the mark of the very opposite of a lowly and humble mind. That is true humility that credits the testimony of God,—that believes because he has spoken it,—that rests in the blood, and righteousness, and all-sufficiency of Jesus, because he has declared that "whoso-ever believeth in him shall be saved." This is genuine lowli-ness,—the blessed product of the Eternal Spirit. To go to Jesus just as I am, a poor, lost, helpless sinner,—to go with-out previous preparation,—to go glorying in my weakness, in-firmity, and poverty, that the free grace and sovereign pleas-ure, and infinite merit of Christ, may be seen in my full par-don, justification, and eternal glory. There is more of un-mortified pride, of self-righteousness, of that principle that would make God a debtor to the creature, in the refusal of a soul fully to accept of Jesus, than is suspected. There is more real, profound humility in a simple, believing venture upon Christ, as a ruined sinner, taking him as all its righteousness, all its pardon, all its glory, than it is possible for any mortal mind to fathom. Doubt is ever the offspring of pride: hu-mility is ever the handmaid of faith.

Nor must we forbear to specify, as among the most fruitful causes of a declension of faith, *the power of unsubdued sin in the heart:* nothing, perhaps, more secretly and effectually militates against the vigour of a life of faith than this. Faith, as we have seen, is a holy, indwelling principle; it has its root in the renewed, sanctified heart; and its growth and fruitful-ness depend much upon the progressive richness of the soil in which it is embedded: if the noxious weeds of the natural soil are allowed to grow and occupy the heart, and gain the ascendancy, this celestial plant will necessarily droop and de-cay. In order to form some conception of the utter incon-gruity of a life of faith with the existence and power of un-mortified sin in the heart, we have but to imagine the case of a believer living in the practice of unsubdued sin. What is the real power of faith in him? where is its strength? where are its glorious achievements? where the trophies it has won in the field of battle? We look for the fruit of faith,—the lowly, humble, contrite spirit—the tender conscience—the travelling daily to the atoning blood—the living upon the grace that is

in Christ Jesus—the carrying out of Christian principle—
crucifixion to the world—patient submission to a life of suffering—meek resignation to a Father's discipline—a living as
beholding Him who is invisible—a constant and vivid realisation of eternal realities,—we look for these fruits of faith; but
we find them not. And why? because there is the worm of
unmortified sin feeding at the root; and until that is slain,
faith will always be sickly, unfruitful, and "ready to die."
"Therefore, brethren, we are debtors, not to the flesh to live
after the flesh. For if ye live after the flesh, ye shall die; but
if ye through the Spirit do mortify the deeds of the body, ye
shall live."

A looking off of Christ will tend greatly to the weakening
and unfruitfulness of faith. It is said, that the eagle's eye
becomes strong through the early discipline of the parent;
placed in such a position when young, as to fix the gaze in-
tently upon the sun, the power of vision gradually becomes so
great, as to enable it in time to look at its meridian splendour
without uneasiness, and to descry the remotest object without difficulty. The same spiritual discipline strengthens the
eye of faith; the eye grows vigorous by looking much at the
Sun of righteousness. The more constantly it gazes upon
Jesus, the stronger it grows; and the stronger it grows, the
more glory it discovers in him, the more beauty in his person,
and perfection in his work. Thus strengthened, it can see
things that are afar off,—the promises of a covenant-keeping
God, the hope of eternal life, the crown of glory—these it can
look upon and almost touch: "Faith is the substance of things
hoped for, the evidence of things not seen." And of the Old
Testament worthies it is recorded by the same Spirit: "These
all died in faith, not having received the promises, but having
seen them afar off, and were persuaded of them, and embraced them, and confessed that they were strangers and
pilgrims on the earth." O precious, costly grace of the Eternal
Spirit! who would not possess thee? who would not mortify

everything that would wound, enfeeble, and cause thee to decay in the soul?

It only remains for us to show in what way the Holy Spirit *revives*, *strengthens*, and *increases* the declining grace of faith. And this he does, in the first place, *by discovering to the believer the cause of its declension, and setting him upon, and strengthening him in, the work of its removal.* The Spirit leads the declining believer to the spiritual duty of *self-examination.* When any grace of the Spirit is in a sickly and declining state, an effect so painful must originate in a cause that needs to be searched out: the great difficulty in a backsliding soul, is, to bring it to the spiritual and needed duty of self-scrutiny. There is something so humiliating, so foreign to the natural inclination of the heart, and withal, to which the very declension of the soul is so strongly opposed, that it requires no little putting forth of the Spirit's grace, to bring the believer honestly and fully into it. Just as the merchant, conscious of the embarrassed state of his affairs, shrinks from a thorough investigation of his books, so does the conscious backslider turn from the honest examination of his wandering heart. But as the cure of any disease, or the correction of any evil, depends upon the knowledge of its cause, so does the revival of a declining believer closely connect itself with the discovery and removal of that which led to his declension. Declining believer, what is the *cause* of thy weak faith? Why is this lovely, precious, and fruitful flower drooping, and ready to die? What has dimmed the eye, and paralysed the hand, and enfeebled the walk of faith? Perhaps it is the *neglect of prayer*: thou hast lived, it may be, days, and weeks, and months, without communion with God; there have been no constant and precious visits to thy closet; no wrestling with God; no fellowship with thy Father. Marvel not, beloved, that thy faith languisheth, droopeth, and fadeth. The greater marvel is, that thou hast any faith at all; that it is not quite dead, plucked up by the root; and but for the mighty power of God, and the constant intercession of Jesus at his right hand, it would long since have ceased to be. But what will revive it?—*An immediate return to prayer;* revisit thy closet; rebuild the broken altar; rekindle the expiring flame; seek thy forsaken God. O how can faith be revived, and how can it grow, in the neglect of daily, secret, and wrestling prayer with God? The Eternal Spirit laying this upon thine heart, showing thee thy awful neglect, and breathing into thee afresh the spirit of grace and supplication, will impart a new and blessed impulse to faith.

Perhaps you have been misinterpreting the Lord's providential dealings with you; you have been indulging in unbelieving, unkind, unfilial views of your trials, bereavements, and disappointments; you have said, "Can I be a child, yet be afflicted thus? can he love me, yet deal with me so?" O that thought! O that surmise! Couldst thou have looked into the *heart* of thy God when he sent that trial, caused that bereavement, blew upon that flower, and blasted that fair design, thou wouldst never have murmured more: so much love, so much tenderness, so much faithfulness, so much wisdom wouldst thou have seen as to have laid thy mouth silent in the dust before him. Wonder not that, indulging in such misgivings, interpreting the covenant dealings of a God of love in such a light, thy faith has received a wound. Nothing perhaps more tends to unhinge the soul from God, engender distrust, hard thoughts, and rebellious feelings, than thus to doubt his loving-kindness and faithfulness in the discipline he is pleased to send. But faith, looking through the dark cloud, rising on the mountain wave, and anchoring itself on the Divine veracity, and the unchangeable love of God, is sure to strengthen and increase by every storm that beats upon it.

Is it the enchantment of the world that has seized upon thy faith? has it stolen upon thee, beguiled thee, caught thee with its glitter, fascinated thee with its syren song, overwhelmed thee with its crushing cares?—Come out from it, and be separ-

ate; resign its hollow friendship, its temporising policy, its
carnal enjoyments, its fleshly wisdom, its sinful conformity.
All these becloud the vision, and enfeeble the grasp of faith.
The world, and the love of it, and conformity to it, may please
and assist the life of *sense*, but it is opposed to, and will re-
tard, the life of *faith*. Not more opposed in their natures are
the flesh and the Spirit, darkness and light, sin and holiness,
than are a vigorous life of faith and a sinful love of the world.
Professor of the Gospel! guard against the world; it is your
great bane: watch against conformity to it in your dress, in
your mode of living, in the education of your children, in the
principles, and motives, and policy, that govern you. We
would say to every professing Christian, be a *non-conformist*
here; separate yourselves from the world,—that world that
crucified your Lord and Master, and would crucify his faith
that is in you; touch not the unclean thing, for, " ye are a
chosen generation, a royal priesthood, an holy nation, a
peculiar people; that ye should show forth the praises of him
who hath called you out of darkness into his marvellous
light." Would you be " strong in faith, giving glory to God?"
—then yield obedience to the voice which, with an unearthly
tongue, exclaims to every professing child of God, " be not
conformed to this world, but be transformed by the renewing
of your mind, that ye may prove what is that good, and acceptable, and perfect will of God!"

Is it unmortified sin that feeds at the root of faith? Bring
it to the cross of Christ,—condemn it there, nail it there, and
leave it not until you are enabled to exclaim, " Thanks be
unto God, who always causeth me to triumph through Christ
Jesus!"

Is it the indulgence of unbelieving and dishonouring fears
touching your interest in Christ? Yield them, and let the
wind scatter them; there is no ground for the doubts and unbelief of a child of God; there may be much in himself to cast
him down, but nothing in the truth which he professes to be-

lieve; there is nothing in the subject-matter of faith, nothing in Christ, nothing in the work of Christ, nothing in the word of God, calculated to beget a doubt or a fear in the heart of a poor sinner. On the contrary, everything to inspire confidence, strengthen faith, and encourage hope. Does his sin plead loud for his condemnation?—the voice of Immanuel's blood pleads louder for his pardon; does his own righteousness condemn?—the righteousness of Christ acquits. Thus there is nothing in Christ to engender an unbelieving doubt in a poor convinced sinner. Himself he may doubt,—he may doubt his ability to save himself,—he may doubt his power to better his condition, to make himself more worthy and acceptable, but never let him doubt that Christ is all that a poor, lost, convinced sinner wants. Let him not doubt that Jesus is the Friend of sinners, the Saviour of sinners, and that he was never known to cast out one who in lowliness and brokenness of heart, sought his compassionate grace. O seek, reader, more simple views of Jesus; clearer views of his great and finished work; take every doubt as it is suggested, every fear as it rises, to him; and remember that whatever of vileness you discover in yourself that has a tendency to lay you low, there is everything in Jesus calculated to lift you from the dunghill, and place you among the princes. Discovering to the backsliding believer these points,—making known to him which it is that causes the declension of his faith, the Eternal Spirit of God takes the first step in the great and precious work of revival.

A further step by which the Holy Spirit revives the decaying faith of the believer is, *by leading him to rest more simply on the faithfulness of God.* What a restorative to drooping faith are these declarations of the Divine word, which represent God as infinitely unchangeable and faithful: "I am the Lord, I change not": "Every good gift and every perfect gift is from above, and cometh down from the Father of lights, with whom is no variableness, neither shadow of turning":

"I will betroth thee unto me in faithfulness": "Righteousness shall be the girdle of his loins, and faithfulness the girdle of his reins": "Nor will I suffer my faithfulness to fail": "Great is thy faithfulness": "Faithful is he that promised!" And then to remember, that the unbelief of the believer never affects the faithfulness of God! "If we believe not, yet he abideth faithful; he cannot deny himself." This is the only true and secure anchorage-ground for a poor soul, tossed amid the waves of doubt and perplexity;—to know that God cannot alter his word,—that it is impossible that he should lie, that were he to deviate from his infinite perfection, he would cease to be a perfect Being, and consequently would cease to be God: to know, too, that he is faithful in the midst of the unfaithfulness and perpetual startings aside of his child,— faithful in the depth of the deepest affliction,—faithful when earthly hopes wither, and human cisterns are broken, and when the soul is led to exclaim, "His faithfulness hath failed!" O what a spring to a tried and drooping faith, is this view which God himself has given of his own glorious and perfect character! It is no small triumph of faith to walk with God, when all is darkness with the soul, and there is no light; to feel amid the roaring of the waves that still he is faithful; that though he slay, yet the soul can trust him; that though he were to take all else away, he would never remove *himself* from his people. O glorious triumph of faith! "Who is among you that feareth the Lord, that obeyeth the voice of his servant, that walketh in darkness, and hath no light? let him trust 'n the name of the Lord, and stay upon his God."

It will tend much to the revival of a tried and drooping faith to remember, that when the Lord is about to impart any peculiar mercy, *there is always a travail of faith for that mercy*. Some of the choicest mercies of the covenant brought into the experience of the believer, come by a travail of faith: it may be a tedious and painful process; faith may be

long and sharply tried, yet the blessing it will bring forth will
more than repay for all the weeping, and suffering, and crying, it has occasioned. Be not surprised, then, at any severe
trial of faith; be sure that when it is thus tried, God is about
to bring your soul into the possession of some great, and perhaps, hitherto unexperienced mercy. It may be a travail of
faith for *spiritual* blessing; and the result may be a deepening
of the work in your heart, increase of spirituality, more
weanedness from creature-trust, and more child-like leaning
upon the Lord; more simple, close, and sanctifying knowledge
of the Lord Jesus. Or, it may be a travail of faith for *temporal*
mercy, for the supply of some want, the rescue from some em-
barrassment, the deliverance out of some peculiar and trying
difficulty; but, whatever the character of the trial of faith be,
the issue is always certain and glorious. The Lord may bring
his child into difficult and strait paths, he may hedge him about
with thorns so that he cannot get out, but it is only to draw
the soul more simply to repose in himself; that, in the extremity, when no creature would or could help, when refuge
failed and no man cared for his soul, that *then* faith should go
out and rest itself in Him who never disowns his own work,
but always honours the feeblest exhibition, and turns his ear
to the faintest cry. " Out of the depths have I cried unto
thee, O Lord. Lord, hear my voice : let thine ears be atten-
tive to the voice of my supplication." " In my distress I
called upon the Lord, and cried unto my God : he heard my
voice out of his temple, and my cry came before him, even
into his ears." " O magnify the Lord with me, and let us
exalt his name together. I sought the Lord, and he heard me,
and delivered me from all my fears." " This poor man cried,
and the Lord heard him; and saved him out of all his troubles."
Here was the severe travail of faith, and here we see the
blessed result. Thus true is God's word, which declares that
" weeping may endure for a night, but joy cometh in the
morning." " He that goeth forth and weepeth, bearing pre-

cious seed, shall doubtless come again with rejoicing, bringing his sheaves with him."

But more,—*the trial of faith is a test of its degree.* We know not what faith we possess, until the Lord calls it into exercise; we may be greatly deceived as to its nature and degree; to walk upon the stormy water, may be thought by us an easy thing; to witness for Christ, no hard matter: but the Lord brings our faith to the test. He bids us come to him upon the water, and then we begin to sink; he suffers us to be assailed by our enemies, and we shrink from the cross; he puts our faith to the trial, and then we learn how little we possess.

The trial of faith is also a test of its *character*; it is the furnace that tries the ore, of what kind it is: it may be brass, or iron, or clay, or perhaps precious gold; but the crucible will test it. There is much that passes for real faith, which is no faith; there is much spurious, counterfeit metal; it is the *trial* that brings out its real character. The true character of Judas was not known until his covetousness was tempted; Simon Magus was not discovered to possess a spurious faith, until he thought to purchase the gift of God with money; Demas did not forsake the apostle, until the world drew him away. Thus solemnly has our Lord unfolded this truth,— " He that received the seed into stony places, the same is he that heareth the word, and anon with joy receiveth it; yet hath he not root in himself, but dureth for a while : for when tribulation or persecution ariseth because of the word, by-and-by he is offended. He also that received seed among the thorns is he that heareth the word; and the care of this world, and the deceitfulness of riches, choke the word, and he becometh unfruitful." But true faith stands the trial; where there is a real work of grace in the heart, no tribulation, or persecution, or power of this world, will ever be able to expel it thence: but if all is chaff, the wind will scatter it : if all is but dross and tinsel, the fire will consume it. Let the humble and tried believer, then, thank God for every test that brings out the real character of his faith, and proves it to be " the faith of God's elect." God will try his own work in the gracious soul; every grace of his own Spirit he will at one time or another place in the crucible; but never will he remove his eye from off it; he will " sit as a refiner," and watch that not a grain of the precious metal is consumed; he will be with his child in all and every affliction; not for one moment will he leave him. Let gratitude rather than murmuring, joy rather than sorrow, attend every test which a loving and faithful Father brings to his own gracious work,—" that the trial of your faith being much more precious than of gold that perisheth, though it be tried with fire, might be found unto praise, and honour, and glory, at the appearing of Jesus Christ."

Be careful of not making a Saviour of faith. There is a danger—and it cannot be too vigilantly guarded against—of substituting the work of the Spirit for the work of Christ; this mistake it is that leads so many of God's saints to look *within*, instead of *without*, themselves for the evidences of their calling and acceptance; and thus, too, so many are kept all their spiritual course walking in a state of bondage and fear, the great question never fully and fairly settled, or, in other words, never *quite sure* of their sonship. The work of Christ is a great and finished work; it is so glorious that it can admit of no comparison, so complete that it can allow of no addition, and so essential that it can give place to no substitution. Precious as is the work of the Holy Ghost in the heart, and essential as it is to the salvation of the soul, yet he who places it where the work of Jesus ought only to be, deranges the order of the covenant, closes up the legitimate source of evidence, and will assuredly bring distress and uncertainty into his soul. " Righteousness, peace, and joy," are the fruit of a full belief in the Lord Jesus Christ; and he who looks for them away from the cross, will meet with disappointment : but they *are* found in Jesus. He who looks away from himself, from his vileness, guiltiness, emptiness, and poverty, fully and believingly unto Jesus, shall know what the forgiveness of sin is, and shall experience the love of God shed abroad in his heart.

If, then, your faith is feeble and tried, be not cast down; faith does not save you. Though it be an instrument of salvation, and as such, is of vast importance, it is but the instrument; the finished work of Immanuel is the ground of your salvation, yea, it is your salvation itself. Then make not a Saviour of your faith; despise it not if it is feeble, exult not in it if it is strong, trample not on it if it is small, deify it not if it is great; such are the extremes to which every believer is exposed. If your faith is feeble and sharply tried, it is no evidence that you are not a believer; but the evidence of your acceptance in the Beloved, *is to arise from Jesus alone*; then let your constant motto be, " looking unto Jesus"; looking to him just as you are; looking unto him when faith is feeble; looking unto him when faith is tried; looking unto him when faith is declining, yea, looking unto him when you fear you have no faith. Look up, tried and tempted soul! Jesus is the Author, the Sustainer, and he will become the Finisher of thy faith. All thou wantest is in him. One glimpse, dim though it be, of his cross,—one touch, trembling though it be, of his garment,—will lift thee from thy lowest depths, lighten thy heaviest burthen, gild thy darkest prospect, and when thou arrivest at Jordan's brink, will bear thee safely through its swellings, and land thee on the sunny and verdant shores of Canaan. Let this be your prayer, urged unceasingly at the throne of grace until it is answered—"Lord, increase my faith"; and then, with holy Paul, you too shall be enabled with humble assurance to exclaim, " I know in whom I have believed, and am persuaded that he is able to keep that which I have committed unto him against that day!"

CHAPTER IV

DECLENSION IN PRAYER

"Thou restrainest prayer before God."—Job xv. 4.

WERE we to select a single characteristic of personal declension more marked than another, we should feel no hesitation in adopting *the decay of the spirit of prayer* as that feature. As prayer is the first evidence of spiritual life in the soul, and its growth in spirituality and vigour marks the healthy and advancing state of that life, so the *declension* of prayer in its spirit, exercise, and enjoyment, is strongly indicative of the decay of real grace in a child of God. We address ourselves to the unfolding of this subject under the solemn conviction, that it is of more general application to professing believers that upon first reflection some would, perhaps, be ready to admit; and that it involves more serious consequences to the spiritual interests of the soul, than any branch of personal declension we have yet considered.

In opening to the reader *the nature of true prayer,*—which seems proper before we consider its declension,—we remark, there are many solemn and affecting things connected with it, which present it as a subject of vast importance. *What is prayer?* It is the communion of the spiritual life in the soul of man with its Divine Author; it is a breathing back the Divine life into the bosom of God from whence it came; it is holy, spiritual, humble converse with God. That was a beautiful remark of a converted heathen,—" I open my Bible, and God talks with me; I close my Bible, and then I talk with

God." Striking definition of true prayer! It is a talking with God as a child talketh with his father, as a friend converseth with his friend: "And the Lord talked with Moses." Let it be remembered, then, that true prayer is the aspiration of a renewed soul towards God; it is the breathing of the Divine life, sometimes in the accents of sorrow, sometimes as the expression of want, and always as the acknowledgment of dependence; it is the looking up of a renewed, afflicted, necessitous, and dependent child to its own loving Father, in all the consciousness of utter weakness, and in all the sweetness of filial trust.

Who is the *object* of prayer? Jehovah, the Lord of heaven and earth; to him, as the Three in One, does true prayer only address itself. He only hath an ear to hear our tale of sorrow, an arm that can succour in time of need, and a heart that can sympathise with our deep necessity. The high and lofty One that inhabiteth eternity, whose name is Holy, who is the Creator and Governor of all worlds, who bears up the pillars of the universe, to whom all the powers in heaven, in earth, and in hell, are subject, he is the glorious Object to whom we address ourselves in prayer.

Not less amazing is the *medium* of prayer; what is it? Not a creature, dependent as ourselves; but the Lord Jesus Christ, the Son of God, equal in might, majesty, and dominion with the Father, and yet the Elder Brother, the Slain Lamb, the Mediator and Surety, the High Priest of his people. Prayer finds acceptance within the veil, only as it is presented in the name of Jesus. The voice that speaks there, in behalf of the lowly suppliant, is the voice of Immanuel's blood; this is the "new and living way," this is the plea that prevails,—this is the argument that moves Omnipotence itself. He who pleads the blood of Jesus in prayer, may have ten thousand tongues all pleading *against* him, but "the blood of Jesus speaks better things," and drowns their every voice. O precious, costly medium of prayer!

Marvellous, too, is the *Author* of prayer; who is he? The apostle informs us: "Likewise the Spirit also helpeth our infirmities; for we know not what we should pray for as we ought; but the Spirit itself maketh intercession for us, with groanings which cannot be uttered." Thus it is the Holy Ghost who begets the desire, indites the petition, and breathes it forth in prayer through Christ to God. What a sublime exercise, then, is prayer! The outgoing of the Divine life in the soul is its nature,—Jehovah its object,—the Lord Jesus its medium,—and the Holy Ghost its author. Thus, the blessed Trinity in Unity is engaged in the great work of a sinner's approach unto God.

Touching the absolute *necessity* of prayer need we enlarge? And yet it must be admitted, that the believer requires constant exhortation to the exercise of this duty. Do we want any stronger evidence of the perpetual tendency to spiritual declension than this,—that the child of God requires repeated stimulus to the sweet and precious privilege of communion with his heavenly Father?—that he needs to be urged by the strongest arguments and the most persuasive motives to avail himself of the most costly and glorious privilege this side of glory? Does it not seem like pleading with a man to live?— reminding him that he must respirate if he would maintain life? Without the exercise of prayer, we tell a child of God, he cannot live; that this is the drawing in of the Divine life, and the breathing of it forth again; that the spiritual nature requires constant supplies of spiritual nourishment; and that the only evidence of its healthy existence is, its constant rising towards God. We tell him, cease to pray, and all your grace withers, all your vigour decays, and all your comfort dies.

But observe how prayer, as a duty, is *enjoined* in God's word: "Call upon me in the day of trouble, I will deliver thee, and thou shalt glorify me." Psalm l. 15. As though the Lord had said, "Call upon me when all is dark, when all is against you; I speak not now of the day of prosperity, of the sunny hour, when thy soul prospers, when thy business prospers, when all things go smooth with thee, and the sky above thee is cloudless, and the sea beneath thee is unruffled; but call upon me *in the day of trouble*, the day of want, the day of adversity, the day of disappointment and of rebuke, the day when friends forsake and the world frowns upon thee, the day of broken cisterns and withered gourds.—Call upon me in the day of trouble, and I will deliver thee." Observe, too, how our dear Lord enjoined this precious duty upon his disciples: "Thou, when thou prayest, enter into thy closet, and, when thou hast shut thy door, pray to thy Father which is in secret." Matt. vi. 6. And observe how he also *encouraged* it: "Verily, verily, I say unto you, whatsoever ye shall ask the Father in my name, he will give it you." John xvi. 23. In harmony with this, is the sweet exhortation of the apostle: "Be careful for nothing; but in everything by prayer and supplication with thanksgiving let your requests be made known unto God." Phil. iv. 6. And what a striking unfolding of the true nature of prayer does the same writer give us in Eph. vi. 18: "Praying always with all prayer and supplication in the Spirit, and watching thereunto with all perseverance and supplication for all saints." The apostle James bears the same testimony: "If any of you lack wisdom, let him ask of God, that giveth to all men liberally, and upbraideth not, and it shall be given him." i. 5.

But we take higher ground than this; we urge the exercise of prayer, not merely as a solemn duty to be observed, but also as a precious *privilege* to be enjoyed. Happy is that believer, when *duties* come to be viewed as *privileges*. What! is it no privilege to have a door of access ever open to God? Is it no privilege when the burthen crushes, to cast it upon One who has promised to sustain? When the corruptions of an unsanctified nature are strong, and temptations thicken, is prayer no privilege then? And when perplexed to know the

path of duty, and longing to walk complete in all the will of
God, and, as a child, fearing to offend a loving Father, is it
then no privilege to have a throne of grace, an open door of
hope? When the world is slowly stealing upon the heart, or
when that heart is wounded through the unkindness of friends,
or is bleeding under severe bereavement, is it then no privilege to go and tell Jesus? Say, ye poor, ye needy, ye tried, ye
tempted souls! say, if prayer is not the most precious, balmy
and costly privilege this side heaven.

And yet, how much infidelity still lingers in the heart of a
renewed soul, touching this solemn duty and immense privilege! That is infidelity that takes a believer in the hour of his
need *first* to the arm of flesh, rather than in prayer to God.
To go to the creature first, is to " go down into Egypt " for
help,—a sin which God has signalised with his severest displeasure.

But true prayer may greatly *decline*; and to the consideration of this point, in connexion with the means of its revival,
we now proceed to direct the serious attention of the reader.

Prayer is the spiritual pulse of the renewed soul; its beat
indicates the healthy or unhealthy state of the believer. Just
as the physician would decide upon the health of the body
from the action of the pulse, so would we decide upon the
spiritual health of the soul before God, by the estimation in
which prayer is held by the believer. If the soul is in a spiritually healthy, growing state, prayer will be vigorous, lively,
spiritual, and constant; if, on the contrary, an incipient process
of declension is going forward in the soul—if the heart is wandering, and love waxeth cold, and faith is decaying, the spirit
and the habit of prayer will immediately betray it.

In the first place, we remark, that the *spirit of prayer* may
decline in the believer, and he may not at once be sensible of
it. The form and the habit of prayer may for a while continue, the domestic altar sustained, and even the closet occasionally visited;—but the spirit of prayer has evaporated, and

all is coldness and dulness, the very torpor and frigidity of death! But of what real worth is the habit of prayer apart from the spirit of prayer? just what this planet would be without the sun, or the body without the living, animating, breathing soul,—what but a cold, lifeless form? Yes; and a believer may be beguiled into this lamentable state, and not a suspicion of its existence be awakened; he may observe his accustomed habit, and use his empty form, and not suspect that all is cold and breathless as death itself. O it is not the rigidly-observed form that God looks at; nor is it great volubility, and eloquent fluency, and rich sentiment, and splendid imagery, and rounded periods, that God regards: far from this. A man may not be able to give expression to his deep emotion in prayer, his thoughts may find no vehicle of utterance, language may entirely fail him; or, if he attempts the audible expression of his wants, there may be much that offends a refined taste, and that grates harshly upon a musical ear, and yet the *spirit of prayer* may glow in his breast;—and this—the true language of prayer—finds its way to the ear and to the heart of God. Now it is manifest from observation, as it is from God's word, that the *spirit* of prayer may depart from a soul, and the *gift* of prayer and its *form* may remain. The form may be found easy,—words, and even thought, may flow freely, and yet, no warmth, no life, no spirituality, no power, no unction, attend the prayer; and this may long continue the state of a professing man. O guard against it, reader; look well to the state of your soul; examine your prayers; see that ye have not substituted the cold *form* for the glowing *spirit*, the mere body for the soul. Real prayer is the breathing of God's own Spirit in the heart; have you *this*? It is *communion* and *fellowship* with God; know you what *this* is? It is brokenness, contrition, confession, and that often springing from an overwhelming sense of his goodness and his love shed abroad in the heart; is *this* thy experience? Again we repeat it, look well to your prayers; test them, not by the natural or acquired *gift* which you may possess,—this is nothing with God; in answer to all your forms, he may say, " I hear no prayer. To what purpose is the multitude of your sacrifices unto me, when ye come to appear before me? who hath required this at your hands to tread my courts? Bring no more vain oblations; incense is an abomination unto me. Your new moons and your appointed feasts my soul hateth; they are a trouble unto me, I am weary to bear them. And when ye spread forth your hands, I will hide mine eyes from you : yea, when ye make many prayers, I will not hear "; but test them by the real communion you have with God,—the returns they make to your soul.

There is yet another state in which *the habit of prayer does not even survive the declension of the spirit of prayer.* There may be instances, in which, as we have just shown, the form may be rigidly sustained long after true prayer has departed from the soul; there may be too much light in the conscience, and too much strength in the force of habit, and something, too, in the appearance of the thing, that will not allow of a total abandonment of this. But, in most cases of actual back-sliding, the habit declines with the spirit; the latter having gone, the former becomes insipid and tedious; and is at last thrown off as a thing irksome and painful to the mind. And yet even the relinquishment of the form is not always a *sudden* act: Satan is too subtle, and the heart too deceitful, to allow of this; there must be steps in the decline. The sudden breaking off from the accustomed habit of prayer might awaken alarm, and surprise, and thoughtfulness : " Has it come to this?" would be the exclamation of the startled soul. " Am I so far gone, as to abandon even my wonted habit of prayer?" Such a pause and such an inquiry might possibly lead to self-examination, contrition, and a return : but the declension is *gradual.* The first habit that is relinquished with the declension of the spirit of prayer, is that of *closet prayer* : this is the first exercise that loses its sweetness, and becomes tedious and insipid, because it is the most spiritual of all devotional exercises, and has most to do with the secret intercourse of the soul with God. And who can portray the loss? No more hallowed visits to the closet; no more turning aside from business, from care, and from the world, to be shut in with God; no more precious, heart-melting, spirit-humbling, heaven-reviving seasons of communion and fellowship with the Father who heareth in secret; no more sweet visits of love from Jesus, nor breathing of the heart's sorrows and wants into his secret ear;—the closet is abandoned, and with it all pleasant, holy, and happy walk with God!

The relinquishment of *ejaculatory prayer* then follows. That holy habit of a growing Christian, which, while in the world, and diligently engaged in its lawful calling, yet keeps him soaring above it; which sustains the wheels of the soul in easy and constant motion, preserves it in a holy, heavenly frame; fortifies it against the surprisals of the adversary, and strengthens it in every inward or outward conflict,—ejaculatory prayer, the " prayer without ceasing," is given up; and all seems a blank between the soul and God!

Family prayer is, perhaps, the next devotional habit that is abandoned. That " border which keeps the web of daily life from unravelling"; that exercise which throws so hallowing an influence around the domestic circle,—cementing the hearts, awakening and concentrating the sympathies, fortifying the mind, and softening the cares and trials of each loved member, is now yielded: the family Bible, so regularly brought out, spread open, read, and expounded, is now laid aside; the altar around which clustered in devout and reverential silence the lowly group, and from which ascended the morning and the evening sacrifice, is thrown down; for he who officiated at its holy shrine, has declined in the spirit of prayer, and the effects of his declension are felt and traced by every member, and through every department of the domestic circle; the patriarch no more returns to bless his household!

Social prayer is now relinquished without a sigh. That service that was once found so refreshing and exhilarating at the close of the day's cares; and which, amid its fatigues, anxieties, and disappointments, was so fondly anticipated and ardently longed for, comes and passes away unheeded and unregretted. The hour of prayer arrives, we look at the vacant place and we inquire, " where is he?"—away, amid the world's turmoil and ardent in its pursuit: " where is he?"—gone, perhaps, to some scene of carnal amusement, folly, and sin; and he, who, when the season of social communion returned, was present to cheer and encourage with his prayers and exhortations the souls of the devout assembly, is now away " sowing to the flesh," and giving to the " things that are temporal," the time and the energies that belong to the " things that are eternal." This is the man in whom the spirit of prayer has declined! From one step of declension he has proceeded to another, until his soul has become, as to all grace and spirituality and love, like the barren heath of the desert, without a spot of verdure to cheer and enliven it. But there are yet other consequences of the soul's declension in the spirit and habit of prayer too solemn and serious to overlook: they are the following:—

A distant walk from God will superinduce *distant thoughts of God*, and this is no light matter. If the simple axiom be true, that the more intimate we become with any object, the better we are prepared to judge of its nature and properties, we may apply it with peculiar appropriateness to our acquaintance with God. The encouraging invitation of his word, is, " Acquaint now thyself with God, and be at peace." Now, it is this *acquaintance* with God that brings us into the knowledge of his character as a holy, loving, and faithful God; and it is this knowledge of his character that begets love and confidence in the soul towards him. The more we *know* of God, the more we *love* him: the more we *try* him, the more we *confide* in him. Let the spiritual reader, then conceive what dire effects must result from a *distant* walk from God. The farther the soul gets from him, the more imperfect must be its knowledge of him. When he appears in his corrective dealings, how will those dealings be interpreted in the distant walk of the soul? As of a covenant God? as of a loving Father? Nay, far from it. They will receive a harsh and unkind interpretation, and this will neutralise their effect: for in order to reap the proper fruit of the Lord's dealings with the soul, it is necessary that they should be viewed in the light of his faithfulness and love. The moment they are otherwise interpreted, the soul starts off from God, and wraps itself up in gloomy and repulsive views of his character, and government, and dealings. But this will assuredly follow from a distant walk. O guard against declension in prayer: let there be no distance between God and thy soul.

A change in the sweetness and enjoyment of spiritual duties, may be regarded as another and painful effect of a declension in this holy exercise: they will become less desired, and more irksome and insipid: will be regarded less as a privilege, more as a burthen and a task. What is the spiritual duty? Is it *meditation*? The mind is not attuned to this. It demands a spiritual mind, one richly anointed of the Holy Ghost, and accustomed to close intercourse with God, rightly and profitably to enjoy it. Is it the *communion of saints*? This soon becomes irksome and insipid. The company of God's humble, broken-hearted people hungering and thirsting for holiness, and seeking crucifixion to the world; the word of God their study, the love of Christ their theme, and Divine conformity their aim, soon loses its attraction to a professing man walking at a distance from God. Yea, we might enumerate all the spiritual duties familiar to the child of God; and not one will be found to possess attraction or sweetness to that soul passing through a process of declension in prayer. Why is it, reader, that meditation, and the research of God's word, and holy intercourse with his saints, and praise, are privileges

dry and tasteless to thy soul? Thou canst turn from them
with loathing. Any engagements but these,—the calls of
business, worldly company, the perusal of a novel, will satisfy
thee! Where art thou? How hast thou declined! It was
not *once* so. O how precious in the first love of thine espousals were the moments of holy abstraction!—how eagerly
sought, and richly enjoyed, was the communion of saints!—
how sweet a privilege was praise, and how sacred a duty was
prayer! Is it all gone? Is it all winter with thee now? No
verdant spot, no green pasture, no still waters? O return
again to prayer! Thy sad distance from God is the secret of
thy soul's leanness. The withering of the spirit of prayer has
withered thy grace, and with it all spiritual enjoyment of the
means.

A falling off in the external deportment of the believer, is a
necessary and often a certain consequence of a declension of
the spirit and habit of prayer. The lowliness, self-oblivion,
softness of walk, and exemplary regard for the honour and
glory of God, of the *prayerful* man, are often succeeded by
loftiness of spirit and of mien, self-confidence, a readiness to
sit in judgment upon the conduct and infirmities of others, a
cold indifference to the increase of the kingdom of Christ and
the conversion of sinners, and a carelessness in the outward
deportment of the *prayerless* man. All backsliding has its
commencement in the declension of prayer: it may date its
beginning at the throne of grace. The restraining of prayer
before God was the first step in departure; and the first step
taken, and not immediately retraced, was quickly succeeded
by others. The path of a backslider from God is always downward: the descent is easy and rapid: the velocity of the soul's
departure increases with its progress; and when a professing
man evinces an inclination and an evidence of spiritual declension, there are not wanting influences ready to assist him
on in his departure. Satan, the subtle and sleepless foe of the
soul, is prepared with a thousand enticements to smooth the

downward path; the world appears with some new attraction; sin tastes less bitter, and appears less "exceeding sinful"; objects of sense become familiar, are looked at, admired, then embraced: and now the soul, but for preserving and restraining grace, has taken a farewell for ever of God. Reader, dost thou tremble at the possibility of ever becoming a backslider? dost thou fear a fall? dost thou dread the thought of wounding Jesus? then, restrain not prayer before God; vigilantly guard against the *first* symptom of declension in this holy exercise, or if that symptom has already appeared, haste thee to the dear Physician, who alone has power to arrest its progress, and heal thy soul.

An accumulation of daily crosses, seldom fails to follow declension in prayer. The constant exercise of prayer makes light every burthen, and smooths every rugged step of a child of God: it is this only that keeps down his trials; not that he is ever exempt from them,—nay, it is "through much tribulation that he is to enter the kingdom";—he is a disciple of the cross, his religion is that of the cross, he is a follower of Him who died upon the cross, and entire exemption from the cross he never expects until he passes to the possession of the crown. But he may *pray down* his crosses: prayer will lessen their number, and will mitigate their severity. The man whose walk is far from God, whose frame is cold, and worldly, and careless, if he be a true child of the covenant, one of the Lord's family, he may expect crosses and trials to increase upon every step he advances towards the kingdom. Ah! little do many of the tried, afflicted, and constantly disappointed believers think, how closely related are these very trials, and afflictions, and disappointments, to their restraining of prayer before God: every step seems attended with some new cross, —every scheme is blasted by some adverse wind,—every effort is foiled,—disappointment follows disappointment, wave attends upon wave,—nothing they attempt prospers, all they enter upon fails,—and everything seems against them. O!

could we pass behind the scene, what should we discover?—a deserted throne of grace! Were we to divulge the secret, and place it in the form of a charge against the believer, what would it be?—"THOU HAST RESTRAINED PRAYER BEFORE GOD!" The scheme was framed *without prayer*; the enterprise was entered upon *without prayer*; the effort was made *without prayer*;—God has blown upon it, and all has come to nought. No marvel; God was not consulted,—the Lord was not acknowledged, his permission was not asked, his wisdom was not sought, his blessing was not craved; and so he blew upon it all! The precious injunction is,—" Trust in the Lord with all thine heart, and lean not unto thine own understanding. In all thy ways acknowledge him, and he shall direct thy paths." Where this is honoured, there is the Divine blessing; where it is slighted, there is the Divine displeasure.

But we need not enlarge; the evils resulting from a declension of prayer are sufficiently obvious. We have shown that the secret of a happy life, and the spring of a holy one, are in a close walk with God; that if a child of God restrains prayer, he opens the door for the departure of every grace, and to the admission of every sin : when these statements have been seriously and prayerfully pondered, let the reader follow us to the consideration of those means which the Lord has appointed and owned, for the REVIVAL of the spirit and exercise of prayer in the believer.

The believer should correctly ascertain the true character of his prayers. Are they lively and spiritual? are they the exercises of the heart, or of the understanding merely? Are they the breathings of the indwelling Spirit, or the cold observance of a form without the power? Is it communion and fellowship? Is it the filial approach of a child, rushing with confidence and affection into the bosom of a Father, and sheltering itself there in every hour of need? It should be remembered by every professing man, that there is a great difference between prayer and praying; we mean, between the formal observance of the duty, and the spiritual character of the performance. All prayer is not communion; and here a man may be greatly and awfully deceived; he may repeat his visits to the throne of grace, and go and come without having exhaled a single breath of spiritual prayer; there may be no respiration in the soul; all is formal, cold, and lifeless. This, then, is the first step to a revival of true prayer in the soul. Examine the character of your devotions; are they such as will stand the test of God's word? will they compare with the holy breathings of David, and Job, and Solomon, and the New Testament saints? are they the breathings forth of the life of God within you? are they ever accompanied with filial brokenness, lowliness of spirit, and humble and contrite confession of sin? See well to your prayers! be not content with half-hearted devotions; be not satisfied with cold, dull, formal petitions. Take care that your *family prayers* degenerate not into this,—there is danger here; see that the flame burns brightly, and rises high on that sacred altar,—that your breathings to God are such as to carry conviction to the minds of your children, your domestics, and your friends, that the duty in which they are engaged is the most spiritual, holy, and solemn of all engagements; they will form their view of prayer by your performance of it at the domestic altar. Be cautious that you beget not in them a disgust for the exercise. If their minds are unregenerate, great wisdom and deep spirituality are needed to guard against this. Let them see that you attach a great and solemn importance to the duty; be not hurried in its performance; let it take precedence of all other engagements; nothing should crowd upon it, and thus curtail the time sacred to it alone. If possible, it should always precede the morning and evening's repast; the mind is thus hallowed with solemn thought, and is better fitted for the varied engagements that follow. It has been found a beneficial practice, too, to supply each member of the domestic circle with a Bible, each in succession reading a verse of the chapter, or else following the individual conducting the devotional exercise. This will prevent the roving eye, and will check distraction of thought, by concentrating the mind upon the portion that is read. An occasional comment, explaining a term, or elucidating a truth, or reconciling an apparent discrepancy, will often impart increased interest and profit to the service. Should there be no godly *father* at the head of the family, let not the Christian *mother* shrink from the discharge of this engagement: the word of God is on her side—the grace of Christ Jesus is on her side—God himself is on her side; let her erect the family altar in the fear of God, and in the strength of Jesus,—around it let her gather her children and her domestics, and let her be the priestess that offers up the morning and the evening sacrifice: it is her solemn duty,—and for the discharge of every duty, the Lord has promised to impart all-sufficient grace. 2 Cor. xii. 9.

A further step in the revival of true prayer is, *to become more thoroughly acquainted with our many and varied necessities.* It is the knowledge of his need that gives true eloquence to the petition of the beggar: a sense of destitution, of absolute want, of actual starvation, imparts energy to his plea, and perseverance in its attainment. His language is, " I must have bread, or I die." This is just what we want the child of God to feel. What is he but a pensioner on God's daily bounty?—what resources has he within himself?—none whatever; and what is he without God?—poor indeed. Now, in proportion as he becomes acquainted with his real case, his utter destitution, he will besiege the throne of grace, and take no denial. He must know his wants, he must know what grace he is deficient in, what easy besetting sin clings to him, what infirmities encompass him, what portion of the Spirit's work is declining in his soul, where he is the weakest and the most exposed to the attacks of the enemy, and what yet he lacks to perfect him in all the will of God; let him examine himself honestly, and know his real condition. This will endear the throne of grace, will stir up the slumbering spirit of prayer, will supply him with errands to God, and give argument, energy, and perseverance to his suit. It was his deep and pressing sense of need, that imparted such boldness and power to the wrestlings of Jacob: " I will not let thee go, except thou bless me "; and the Lord said, " Thy name shall be called no more Jacob, but Israel; for as a prince hast thou *power with God* and with men, and hast *prevailed*." Thus imitate the patriarch; begin the day with thinking over what you may possibly need before its close; whether any cross is anticipated, or any temptation is apprehended, or any danger to which you may be exposed; and then go and wrestle for the needed and the promised grace. O it is a great mercy to have an errand that sends us to God; and when we remember what a full heart of love he has, what a readiness to hear, what promptness in all his answers, what entering into the minutest circumstance of a believer's history,—how it chides the reluctance and rebukes the unbelief that we perpetually manifest in availing ourselves of this most costly, holy, and precious of all our privileges!

There should be the searching out and the removal of that which hinders prayer. Many things weaken true prayer: unsubdued sin—unrepented sin—unpardoned sin, we mean the secret sense of it upon the conscience—worldly-mindedness—light and trifling conversation, vain disputations, much and frequent intercourse either with unconverted individuals or cold and formal professors; all these combined, or any single one, will, if suffered to prevail, unfit the mind for converse with God, and cause a decay of the spirit of prayer in the soul. Regard that as injurious which touches the devotional frame of your mind; which abridges the hour of prayer, and removes the fine edge of its holy enjoyment.

But that for which we most earnestly plead, and which will tend more than all beside to the revival of true prayer in the believer, is, *a more enlarged communication of the Holy*

Spirit's gracious influence. Here lies the grand source and secret of all true, spiritual, believing, persevering, and prevailing prayer; it is the lack of this that is the cause of the dulness, and formality, and reluctance, that so frequently mark the exercise. The saints of God honour not sufficiently the Spirit in this important part of his work; they too much lose sight of the truth, that of all true prayer he is the Author and the Sustainer; and the consequence is, and ever will be, self-sufficiency and cold formality in the discharge, and ultimate neglect of the duty altogether. But, let the promise be pleaded, " I will pour upon the house of David, and upon the inhabitants of Jerusalem, the Spirit of grace and of supplication "; let the Holy Ghost be acknowledged as the Author, and constantly sought as the Sustainer of this holy exercise; let the saint of God *feel* that he knows not what he should pray for as he ought, that the Spirit itself maketh intercession for us with groanings which cannot be uttered, and that God knows the mind of the Spirit, because he maketh intercession for the saints according to his will; and what an impulse will this give to prayer! what new life will it impart, what mighty energy, what unction, and what power with God! Seek, then, with all your blessings, this, the richest and the pledge of all, *the baptism of the Spirit*; rest not short of it; you are nothing as a professing man without it; your religion is lifeless, your devotion is formal, your spirit is unctionless; you have no moral power with God or with man, apart from the baptism of the Holy Ghost; seek it, wrestle for it, agonise for it, as transcendently more precious than every other mercy. Submerged in his quickening and reviving influences, what a different Christian will you be! how differently will you pray, how differently will you live, and how differently will you die! Is the spirit of prayer languishing? is its exercise becoming irksome? is closet devotion abandoned? is the duty in any form becoming a task?—O rouse thee to the seeking of the baptism of the Spirit! this alone will stay the progress of thy declension, this will revive the true spirit of prayer within thee, and this will give to its exercise sweetness, pleasantness, and power. God has promised the bestowment of the blessing, and he will never disappoint the soul that seeks it.

The outpouring of the Spirit of prayer, too, is needed to give frequency, and life, and directness, to our petitions *on behalf of the church and the world*. The word of God is explicit on this point. *Thus for all classes and conditions of men:* " I exhort, therefore, that first of all, supplications, prayers, intercessions, and giving of thanks, be made for all men; for kings, and for all that are in authority; that we may live a quiet and peaceable life in all godliness and honesty. For this is good and acceptable in the sight of God our Saviour." 1 Tim. ii. 1-3. And thus, too, *for the church of Christ*: " Pray for the peace of Jerusalem: they shall prosper that love thee." Psalm cxxii. 6. *Intercessory prayer one for the other* is urged: " Confess your faults one to another, and pray one for another, that ye may be healed. The effectual fervent prayer of a righteous man availeth much." James v. 16. And also *for the ministers of the Gospel*: " Brethren, pray for us." Heb. xiii. 18. These are solemn injunctions: who can read them without a secret consciousness of having slighted or overlooked them? But what is to give intensity, and power, and fixedness, and prevalency, to our prayers for the church of Christ, and in behalf of a world still under the dominion and supremacy of sin, but *a large effusion of the Spirit of prayer*? Contracted will be our sympathies, selfish our desires, and cold and general our petitions, if not baptized in the Spirit of prayer. The Holy Ghost, descending as on the day of Pentecost, filling, overwhelming, and saturating us with his influence, O how will the pressing necessities of the church and the moral claims of the world then rise before us in all their eloquent pleadings! We will close the present chapter with a few remarks of a practical tendency.

In all true prayer, *great stress should be laid on the blood of Jesus.* Perhaps no evidence distinguishes a declension in the power and spirituality of prayer more strongly than an overlooking of this. Where the atoning blood is kept out of view; not recognised, not pleaded, not wrestled with, not made the grand plea, there is a deficiency of power in prayer. Words are nothing, fluency of expression nothing, niceties of language and brilliancy of thought nothing, and even apparent fervour nothing, where the blood of Christ,—the new and living way of access to God, the grand plea that moves Omnipotence, that gives admission within the holy of holies,—is slighted, undervalued, and not made the groundwork of every petition. Oh, how much is this overlooked in our prayers,— how is the atoning blood of Immanuel slighted! how little mention we hear of it in the sanctuary, in the pulpit, in the social circle; whereas it is this that makes prayer what it is with God! All prayer is acceptable with God, and only so, as it comes up perfumed with the blood of Christ; all prayer is answered as it urges the blood of Christ as its plea : it is the blood of Christ that satisfies justice, and meets all the demands of the law against us; it is the blood of Christ that purchases and brings down every blessing into the soul; it is the blood of Christ that sues for the fulfilment of his last will and testament, every precious legacy of which comes to us solely on account of his death. This it is, too, that gives us boldness at the throne of grace,—" Having boldness to enter into the holiest by the blood of Jesus." How can a poor sinner dare approach without this? how can he look up, how can he ask, how can he present himself before a holy God, but as he brings in the hand of faith the precious blood of Jesus? Out of Christ, God can hold no communication with us; all intercourse is suspended, every avenue of approach is closed, all blessing is withheld. God hath crowned his dearly beloved Son, and he will have us crown him too; and never do we place a brighter crown upon his blessed head, than when we plead his finished righteousness as the ground of our acceptance, and his atoning blood as our great argument for the bestowment of all blessing with God. If, then, dear reader, you feel yourself to be a poor, vile, unholy sinner; if a backslider, whose feet have wandered from the Lord, in whose soul the spirit of prayer has declined, and yet still feel some secret longing to return, and dare not, because so vile, so unholy, so backsliding; yet you may return, "having boldness to enter into the holiest by the blood of Jesus." Come, for the blood of Christ pleads; return, for the blood of Christ gives you a welcome: "If any man sin, we have an advocate with the Father, Jesus Christ the righteous."

Forget not that *the season of trial and of bereavement* is often the sanctified occasion of a revival of prayer in the soul. The Lord has marked your wanderings: he has had his eye upon the declension of your soul. That voice, always so pleasant to his ear, has ceased to call upon him: and now he would recover thee; he would hear that voice again. And how will he effect it? He causes you to "pass under the rod," sends some sore trial, lays on thee some weighty cross, brings trouble and sorrow into thy soul, and then thou criest unto him, and dost besiege the mercy-seat. O how eagerly is God sought, how attractive and how precious does the throne of grace become, when the soul is thus led into deep waters of trial! No longer silent, no longer dumb, the believer calls upon God, pleads with "strong crying and tears," wrestles and agonises, and thus the slumbering spirit of prayer is stirred up and revived in the soul. O sweet affliction, O precious discipline, that brings back the wandering soul to a closer and a holier walk with God!

Again we exhort the believer, guard against the least declension in prayer; let the first unfavourable symptom that appears alarm you; go to the Lord in your *worst* frames; stay not from him until you get a good one. Satan's grand argument to keep a soul from prayer, is—"Go not with that cold and insensible frame; go not with that hard and sinful heart;

stay until you are more fit to approach God." And listening to this specious reasoning, many poor, distressed, burthened, longing souls have been kept from the throne of grace, and consequently from all comfort and consolation. But the Gospel says,—" Go in your very worst frames"; Christ says, —" Come just as you are": and every promise and every example but encourages the soul to repair to the cross whatever be its frame or condition.

CHAPTER V

DECLENSION IN CONNEXION WITH DOCTRINAL ERROR

" Sanctify them through thy truth."—John xvii. 17.

GOD has been graciously pleased to appoint his church the great conservator of his truth, and his truth the especial medium of sanctification to his church; there is a close and beautiful relation between the two. The church may be compared to the golden lamp which contains the sacred oil, which, in its turn, feeds the flame of its light and holiness. The church is to guard with a jealous and vigilant eye the purity of the truth, while the truth is to beautify and sanctify the ark which preserves it; compare 1 Tim. iii. 15; John xvii. 17. Thus there is a close relation, and a reciprocal influence constantly existing and exerted, between the church of Christ and the truth of God.

To this thought add yet another : every individual believer in Jesus is himself a subject, and therefore a witness, of the truth; he has been quickened, called, renewed, and partially sanctified through the instrumentality of God's revealed truth : " Of his own will begat he us with the word of truth." James i. 18. " For the truth's sake which dwelleth in us." 2 John 2. " Ye are my witnesses, saith the Lord." Here is unfolded one of the most solemn and affecting truths touching the character and individual responsibility of a child of God. He is a subject of truth, he is a repository of the truth, and he is a witness for the truth; yea, he is the only living witness to the truth which God has on earth. The world he lives in is a dark, polluted, God-blaspheming, Christ-denying, truth-despising world. The saints who have been called out of it according to his eternal purpose and love, and by his sovereign, distinguishing, and free grace, are the only lights and the only salt in the midst of this moral darkness and corruption. Here and there a light glimmers, irradiating the gloomy sphere in which it moves; here and there a spot of verdure appears, relieving the arid and barren desolation by which it is surrounded. These are the saints of the Most High, the witnesses of the Divine character, the omnipotent power, and the holy tendency of God's blessed truth. Let the saints of God, then, solemnly weigh this affecting fact, that though the written word and the accompanying Spirit are God's witnesses in the world, yet *they* are the only living exemplifications of the power of the truth, and, as such, are earnestly exhorted to be " blameless and harmless, the sons of God without rebuke, in the midst of a crooked and perverse nation, among whom ye shine as lights in the world." Phil. ii. 15.

The first point on which it is our duty to touch in opening the subject of this chapter, is *the holy tendency of Divine truth, or the intimate relation between truth and holiness.* There are two admitted axioms in every department of human science, which will apply with equal force to the matter before us;—viz., that an effect cannot exist without a cause, and that a cause does not operate without the use of means. Let these admitted propositions form the basis of our reasoning upon this important subject. God has designed the sanctification of his people; he has appointed his truth as the great instrument of effecting their sanctification; and in order to accomplish this, he has declared, that his truth must dwell in the heart in the same richness, fulness, and purity with which it is revealed in his word.

In sustaining our proposition, that the truths of the Gospel are the grand means which God employs for the sanctification of his people, let us be distinctly understood in the outset, as disclaiming all belief in the mere power of the truth itself to produce holiness. This is one of the grand errors of modern divinity from which we unhesitatingly dissent, and which we sternly repudiate. The mere presentation of truth to the unrenewed mind, either in the form of threatening, or promise, or motive, can never produce any saving or sanctifying effect. The soul of man in its unrenewed state, is represented as spiritually dead; insensible to all holy, spiritual motion. Now upon such a mind, what impression is to be produced by the mere holding up of truth before its eye? What life, what emotion, what effect will be accomplished? As well might we spread out the pictured canvas before the glazed eye of a corpse, and expect that by the beauty of the design, and the brilliancy of the colouring, and the genius of the execution, we would animate the body with life, and heave the bosom with emotion, and cause the eye to swim with delight, as to look for similar moral effects to result from the mere holding up to view Divine truth before a carnal mind, " dead in trespasses and sins." And yet there are those who maintain the doctrine, that Divine truth, unaccompanied by any extraneous power, can effect all these wonders! Against such a theory we would simply place one passage from the sacred Word : " Except a man be born again, he cannot *see* the kingdom of God."

But the power of the truth for which we plead, is that which results from the attending energy and demonstration of the Holy Spirit. The sacred Word, inspired though it be, is but a dead letter, unclothed with the life-giving power of the Holy Ghost. Awful as are the truths it unfolds, solemn as are the revelations it discloses, touching as are the scenes it portrays, and persuasive as are the motives it supplies, yet, when left to its own unaided operation, Divine truth is utterly impotent to the production of spiritual life, love, and holiness in the soul of man. Its influence must necessarily be passive, possessing as it does no actual power of its own, and depending upon a Divine influence extraneous from itself, to render its teaching efficacious. The three thousand who were converted on the day of Pentecost, were doubtless awakened under one sermon, and some would declare it was the power of the truth which wrought those wonders of grace. With this we perfectly agree, only adding, that it was truth in the mighty hand of God which pricked them to the heart, and wrung from them the cry, " Men and brethren, what shall we do?" The Eternal Spirit was the efficient cause, and the preached truth but the instrument employed, to produce the effect; but for his accompanying and effectual power, they would, as multitudes do now, have turned their backs upon the sermon of Peter, though it was full of Christ crucified, deriding the truth, and rejecting the Saviour of whom it spake. But it pleased God, in the sovereignty of his will, to call them by his grace, and this he did by the effectual, omnipotent power of the Holy Spirit, through the instrumentality of a preached gospel.

Thus, then, we plead for a personal experimental acquaintance with, and reception of, the truth, ere it can produce anything like holiness in the soul. That it has found an entrance to the judgment merely, will not do; advancing not further,—arresting not the will, touching not the heart, renewing not the whole soul,—it can never erect the empire of holiness in man; the reign of sanctification cannot have commenced. The mental eye may be clear, the moral eye closed; the mind all light, the heart all dark; the creed orthodox, and the whole life at variance with the creed. Such is the discordant effect of Divine truth, simply settled in the human understanding, unaccompanied by the power of the Holy Ghost in the heart. But let a man receive the truth in his heart by the power of God himself; let it enter there, disarming and dethroning the strong man; let Jesus enter, and the Holy Spirit take possession, renewing, sealing, and sanctifying the soul; and then we may look for the "fruits of holiness which are unto eternal life."

Now that it is the natural tendency of Divine truth thus received into the heart, to produce holiness, a moment's reference to the word of God will show. The *design* of the whole plan of redemption, was to secure the highest holiness and happiness of the creature; and when the gospel comes with the power of God unto the salvation of the soul, this end is preeminently secured. The renewed man is a pardoned man; the pardoned man becomes a holy man; and the holy man is a happy man. Look, then, at God's word, and trace the tendency of every doctrine, precept, promise, and threatening, and mark the holy influence of each. To select, for example, a few of the distinguishing doctrines of grace. Take the doctrine of God's *everlasting love to his people, as seen in their election to eternal life*. How holy is the tendency of this truth! "Blessed be the God and Father of our Lord Jesus Christ, who hath blessed us with all spiritual blessings in heavenly places in Christ: according as he hath chosen us in him before the foundation of the world, *that we should be holy and without blame before him in love*." Eph. i. 3, 4. Let not my reader turn from this glorious doctrine, because he may find it irreconcilable with others that he may hold, or because the mists of prejudice may long have veiled it from his mind; it is a *revealed* doctrine, and therefore to be fully received; it is a *holy* doctrine, and therefore to be ardently loved. Received in the heart by the teaching of the Holy Ghost, it lays the pride of man in the dust, knocks from beneath the soul all ground for self-glorying, and expands the mind with the most exalted views of the glory, grace, and love of Jehovah. He who receives the doctrine of electing love in his heart by the power of the Spirit, bears about with him the material of a holy walk; its tendency is to humble, abase, and sanctify the man.

Thus holy, too, is the revealed doctrine of God's *free, sovereign, and distinguishing grace.* The tendency of this truth is most sanctifying: for a man to feel that God alone hath made him to differ from another—that what he has he has received—that by the free, distinguishing grace of God, he is what he is,—is a truth, when experienced in the heart, surely of the most holy influence. How it lays the axe at the root of self! how it stains the pride of human glory, and hushes the whispers of vain boasting! It lays the renewed sinner, where he ought ever to lie, in the dust; and places the crown, where it alone ought to shine, bright and glorious, upon the head of sovereign mercy. "Lord, why me? I was far from thee by wicked works; I was the least of my Father's house, and of all, the most unworthy and unlikely object of thy love: and yet thy mercy sought me,—thy grace selected me out of all the rest, and made me a miracle of its omnipotent power. Lord, to what can I refer this, but to thy mere mercy, thy sovereign and free grace, entirely apart from all worth or worthiness that thou didst see in me? Take, therefore, my body, soul, and spirit, and let them be, in time and through eternity, a holy temple to thy glory." Thus "the grace of God, that bringeth salvation, hath appeared to all men, teaching us, that, denying ungodliness and worldly lusts, we should live soberly, righteously, and godly in this present evil world." And so might we pass on through all the kindred doctrines of grace, were it necessary, showing that the *sanctification* of the believer is their great end and tendency.

All the *precepts*, too, are on the side of holiness. "If ye love me, keep my commandments"; "Love not the world, nor the things of the world"; "Come out of the world, and be ye separate, and touch not the unclean thing"; "Watch and pray"; "Pray without ceasing"; "Love as brethren"; "Be ye holy, for I am holy"; "God hath not called us unto uncleanness, but unto holiness"; "That ye might walk worthy of the Lord unto all pleasing, being fruitful in every good work, and increasing in the knowledge of God." Holy precepts! May the Eternal Spirit engrave them deep upon our hearts!

Not less sanctifying in their tendency are those " exceeding great and precious *promises*" which the word of truth contains. " Having, therefore, these promises, dearly beloved, let us cleanse ourselves from all filthiness of the flesh and spirit, perfecting holiness in the fear of God."

Equally holy is the tendency of the Divine *threatenings*. " The day of the Lord will come as a thief in the night; in the which the heavens shall pass away with a great noise, and the elements shall melt with fervent heat, the earth also and the works that are therein shall be burned up. Seeing, then, that all these things shall be dissolved, what manner of persons ought ye to be in all holy conversation and godliness! Nevertheless we, according to his promise, look for new heavens and a new earth, wherein dwelleth righteousness. Wherefore, beloved, seeing that ye look for such things, be diligent that ye may be found of him in peace, without spot, and blameless." Thus holy and sanctifying are the nature and the effect of Divine truth. It is in its nature and properties most holy; it comes from a holy God; and whenever and wherever it is received in the heart, as the good and incorruptible seed of the kingdom, it produces that which is in accordance with its own nature,—HOLINESS. As is the tree, so are the fruits; as is the cause, so are the effects. It brings down and lays low the high thoughts of man, by revealing to him the character of God; it convinces him of his deep guilt and awful condemnation, by exhibiting the Divine law; it unfolds to him God's hatred of sin, his justice in punishing and his mercy in pardoning it, by unfolding to his view the cross of Christ; and taking entire possession of the soul, it implants new principles, supplies new motives, gives a new end, begets new joys, and inspires new hopes,—in a word, diffuses itself through the whole moral man, changes it into the same image, and transforms it into "an habitation of God through the Spirit."

Now it will require no laboured or lengthened discussion to show, that the nature and tendency of *error* must be opposite to that of truth; for it is impossible that two things so different in their natures should be capable of producing the same effects. If the nature and the tendency of *truth* are to promote holiness, it must be the nature and tendency of *error* to promote unholiness: if the one tends to humble the pride of man, to diminish him in his own eyes, to correct the evils of his fallen nature, to break the power of corruption, and to introduce him into the holy liberty of the child of God,—for "if the truth makes him free, then is he free indeed,"—surely the other tends to foster his proud conceit of himself, to beget a lofty view of his own gifts and attainments, to lessen his views of sin's exceeding sinfulness, and, lowering the motive and weakening the power of holiness, gives the unchecked rein to all the corrupt propensities of a fallen nature.

It is the tendency of false doctrine to divert the mind that cherishes it into a wrong channel: it leads the soul away from God. As truth experimentally received draws the heart *to* God, so error cherished in the mind leads the heart *from* God. It imparts distorted views of the Divine character, gives low conceptions of the Divine law, beclouds the finished work of Christ, weakens the power of moral obligation, and, from step to step, leads the soul entirely, and, if grace do not interfere, for ever, from God.

That the connexion between spiritual and personal declension and false doctrine is close and inseparable, and the results always the most painful and disastrous, cannot be questioned. The moment a private Christian, or a public teacher, or an associated body, becomes infected with false doctrine, departs from the word of God, and sets up doctrines, and commandments, and ordinances, at variance with the revealed word, that moment finds him or them deteriorating in spirituality and declining in holiness; and from a career of spiritual prosperity, perhaps the most unexampled, relapsing into a state of formality, deadness, and unfruitfulness, from which nothing seems fully and permanently to recover them.

Select an individual believer, a minister, or the case of a church, which has departed from the "faith once delivered unto the saints," and has relinquished some of the fundamental doctrines of the Gospel, and how marked and painful are the results!

Take, for example, the case of an *individual believer*. Has he abandoned the ancient landmark of truth? Has he lost a reverence for its character, a sense of its value, a relish for its sweetness? Trace the sad effects in his uneven walk, his careless spirit, his low-toned spirituality, his hardened conscience, his insensible heart, his neglect of means—in a word, the apparent withering up of all his grace. What a change has passed over the man! what a distant spirit now marks him whose walk was once so close with God! what exhibitions of self in him who was once so humble and so retiring, whose carriage did seem to speak the inward consciousness of the soul "less than the least of all saints!" what a turning of the back upon the means of grace by him to whom they were once so highly prized, so eagerly sought, so richly enjoyed, amid which he walked as through green pastures, and by the side of still waters! what unkindness, what haughty bearing, what frigid distance, now marks his conduct towards the saints of God, once so dear to his heart, his chosen and beloved companions, with whom he desired to live and to die! He has departed from the faith, and these are some of the dire effects!

Take the still more affecting case of a professed *minister of the Gospel*. Has any change taken place in his views of the

Christian system? has he relinquished any fundamental doctrine of the Gospel? has he abandoned any essential element of revealed truth? Perhaps he has given up the Godhead of Christ, the sacrificial character of his death; or, it may be, he denies the Deity and Personality of the Spirit; or else his views touching the obligation of the believer to holiness have undergone a painful alteration. But, whatever be the error he has imbibed, whether doctrinal or preceptive, a fearful blight has in consequence fallen upon the man. How changed the spiritual frame of his mind!—no more zeal, tenderness, or solemnity marks him. How altered the character of his ministry!—no more power, earnestness, or spirituality, clothes it. How different its results!—no more conversions, and no more edification, comfort, and establishing of the saints, follow it. How differently he prays,—no more unction, life, and power breathe in his petitions. He has imbibed error, he has turned his back upon God's truth, and God has turned his back upon him.

We might go on to trace the same or similar effects, showing the close connexion between false doctrine and spiritual declension, in the history of *a church* which has departed from the purity of the faith; but sufficient has been advanced, we believe, to illustrate the awful consequences of tampering with God's word, and of relinquishing our hold upon a single truth which he has revealed for the sanctification and salvation of the soul.

The inquiry appropriately suggests itself here,—how far may the prevailing deficiency in spirituality be traced to the influence of lax views of Divine truth among professedly orthodox Christians, and to the existence of alarming errors, which, like a flood, threaten to sweep away the ancient landmarks of Gospel truth? That such a dearth of spirituality does exist,—traced in the pulpit, on the platform, from the press, and in the social intercourse of Christians, cannot be doubted: the only question is, To what are we to refer it as a cause? We unhesitatingly reply, To a defective theology, to false doctrine, to low and lax views of God's revealed truth. Declension in spirituality has ever followed a departure from the purity of the faith. Look at the reformed churches on the continent of Europe; they departed from the pure doctrines of the Reformation, and what and where are they now? Scattered, many of them, to the winds,—torn up by the roots; while those that remain have sunk into a state of the deepest declension, abandoned to the withering influence of an infidel neology, and a mystic transcendentalism. It is true, the sun of the Reformation appears in some parts of the land of Calvin and Luther to be emerging from its long and deep obscuration, inspiring hopes of the revival of a more pure and spiritual Christianity. And to what are these favourable symptoms to be traced, save to a return of some of the churches and pastors to the pure doctrines of the Reformation?—doctrines which Luther boldly preached, on which Calvin powerfully wrote, and for which Latimer, Ridley, and Cranmer went fearlessly to the stake. It is much to be feared, that if the reformed churches of England and of America return not soon to a purer and a more spiritual theology, they will smite upon the rocks on which the continental churches have so sadly made shipwreck of faith. To descend to particulars:

Is there not in the present day a criminal keeping back by some, and a painful undervaluing by others, of *the scriptural and holy doctrines of grace?*—The doctrines which unfold the eternity of God's love to his people—the sovereignty of his grace in their election—the effectual power of the Spirit in their calling—the free justification of their persons through the imputed righteousness of Christ, and the entire putting away of their sins by his atoning blood—the solemn obligation to "live soberly, righteously, and godly in this present evil world," and the certainty of their final glorification in the world to come,—are not these Divinely-revealed truths, at the present moment, and by the great mass of Christian professors and preachers, excluded from our pulpits and exiled from our land? are they not considered mean and unfashionable? and, having lost their savour with the many, are they not cast out and trodden under foot of men? We verily and solemnly believe that it is so. By some they are professedly received, but criminally held back; by others they are professedly preached, but with such timidity and obscurity, as to render them of none effect: and by the many they are disbelieved altogether, and therefore openly and boldly denied! And yet, these are the doctrines which shine so luminously in every page of the apostle's writings,—these are the doctrines which formed the grand themes of Christ's ministration,—and these are the doctrines, to the preaching of which by the reformers, we owe all the civil and religious liberty which, as a nation, we now possess. We hesitate not, then, to say that, along with the denial or the undervaluing of these doctrines of grace, there will go forth an influence that will wither the spirituality and obstruct the prosperity of the churches of our land. It is true, an outward appearance of fruitfulness may follow the exhibition of opposite and conflicting doctrines,—crowds may flock to their standard, and multitudes seem converted by their influence,—but soon these delusive appearances are seen to pass away. The time of trial and of sifting comes, and then it is found—when, alas! too late to close the floodgate against the overwhelming evils which the preaching of error has produced—that the truth, and the truth only, in the hands of the Eternal Spirit of God, can really enlighten the dark mind, regenerate the lifeless soul, and subdue and sanctify the rebellious heart: it is then discovered, that the true prosperity of a church, its stability, its spirituality, its vigour, and its holy influence, are essentially, and therefore inseparably, connected with a fearless and holy maintenance of the doctrines of grace; that where they are denied, or held back, or in any way obscured, there may indeed exist the *form* of godliness, but the power—the glorious, Divine, and sanctifying *power*—is wanting. The preaching of false doctrine may build up a church composed of "wood, hay, stubble," but the preaching of *truth* alone can rear a church composed of "gold, silver, precious stones." And the day is approaching, when "every man's work shall be made manifest; for the day shall declare it, because it shall be revealed by fire; and the fire shall try every man's work of what sort it is." 1 Cor. iii. 13.

Do we long, and pray, and labour for a true revival of the Lord's work?—What is more calculated to bring down the Holy Spirit of God upon us in all the plenitude of his awakening influence,—arousing the careless, convincing the impenitent and unbelieving of sin, annihilating the self-righteousness, prostrating the high thoughts, and slaying the pride of the human heart,—than a clear, pointed, and faithful exhibition of God's own revealed truth? Has not the great experiment been tried, and the question set at rest?—It has. President Edwards, in his *Narrative of Surprising Conversions*, bears this testimony:—"I think I have found," says he, "that no discourses have been more remarkably blessed than those in which the doctrine of God's absolute sovereignty with regard to the salvation of sinners, and his just liberty with regard to his answering the prayers, or succeeding the pains of mere natural men, continuing such, have been insisted on. I never found so much immediate saving fruit, in any measure, of any discourses I have offered to my congregation, as some from those words, 'That every mouth may be stopped,' Rom. iii. 19; endeavouring from thence to show, that it would be just with God for ever to reject and cast off mere natural men."

And to go still further back in search of a stronger testimony; what was the great revival at Jerusalem on the day of Pentecost the result of, but a faithful exhibition of the *truth*, brought to bear upon the consciences and the hearts of three thousand rebellious sinners, by the bold apostle Peter? The doctrines he then proclaimed, were the now despised and slighted *doctrines of grace*; the truths he then thundered forth, were the most humbling to human pride, and the most offensive to the natural heart, and yet the most calculated, in the hands of the Eternal Spirit, to awaken the deepest emotion, and to produce the most anxious inquiry:— " Him, being delivered by the determinate counsel and foreknowledge of God, ye have taken, and by wicked hands have crucified and slain." "Now, when they heard this, they were pricked in their heart, and said unto Peter and the rest of the apostles, Men and brethren, what shall we do?" This was the result of a simple preaching of the truth,—a faithful exhibition of the doctrines of grace. The stout-hearted Jews listened with awe : the men who had witnessed the awful scene of Calvary without emotion, now quailed, trembled, turned pale, and smote on their breasts, in all the anguish of a deep, pungent conviction of sin. How soon did their proud natures bend, their hard hearts melt; the strong fortress of their prejudices yield before the simplicity and the majesty of the truth! It was the naked " sword of the Spirit" which Peter wielded, and this, at one blow, smote to the earth three thousand of the most hopeless, impenitent sinners; it was a crucified Saviour that he held up, which, by the power of the Holy Ghost, wrought the wonders of the day of Pentecost. " Is not my word," saith God, " like as a fire, and like a hammer that breaketh the rock in pieces?" " Thine arrows are sharp in the hearts of the king's enemies, whereby the people fall under thee." Is it unreasonable, then, to expect, that the same Spirit will honour with similar tokens of his power, the preaching of the same truths in our day? " Thus saith the Lord, Stand ye in the ways and see, and ask for the old paths, where is the good way, and walk therein, and ye shall find rest for your souls." Jer. vi. 16.

We would also inquire, is there not in the present day a sad declension *in the setting forth of the Lord Jesus Christ?* Have we not cause to sound the note of alarm touching this most important point? We verily and solemnly believe that the pulpits of our land are awfully guilty here; that the modern preaching of the Gospel is not formed on the model of the apostles', which was—Christ crucified: " I determined not to know (or to make known) anything among you, save Jesus Christ, and him crucified." Is not Jesus kept in the background? Is not his cross hidden, and much of his glory veiled, as if ashamed to bring him fully forward? Are the glory, the majesty, and the beauty of his Divine and human nature, his wondrous person, clearly set forth? Are the nature, necessity, and perfection of his great work, fully and fearlessly unfolded? Are his precious blood, his imputed righteousness, his mediatorial fulness, his exaltation and intercession at the right hand of God, truths prominently exhibited and fervently preached? On the contrary, are not human knowledge, and splendid talents, and brilliant eloquence, and moral suasion, greatly substituted for the preaching of the cross? That there should be a sad declension of vital piety, of real spirituality, and of active exertion, where Christ is not fully preached, is not to be wondered at. The cross of Jesus is the very soul of Christianity; all is death where Jesus is not. Grace decays, piety languishes, and formality takes the place of the power of the Gospel, where the person and the work of Christ are slighted, undervalued, or denied. How we should pray that the Lord Jesus Christ, the Lamb slain, who is " worthy to receive power, and riches, and wisdom, and strength, and honour, and glory, and blessing," should be more fully and simply preached through the length and breadth of our land; that the church and the pulpit should more manifestly crown him Lord of all!

Once more: Is not the doctrine of the Holy Spirit held slightly? Is he not denied in his person, dishonoured in his work, wounded and grieved in his influence? Is there not a more marked dependence on creature power than upon the power of the Spirit? Do not sermons, and books, and reports sadly forget to recognise and honour him as the grand source of all blessing? Are his power, grace, and love, in the great work of conversion, distinctly acknowledged and duly honoured? That there should be no precious gales of grace, no revival of the Lord's work, no true spiritual prosperity where the Holy Spirit is not glorified, we cannot marvel. All must be cold, formal, and lifeless—that church a stagnant pool, and that ministry a powerless instrument, where the Spirit of God is slighted, wounded, or absolutely denied.

In closing, let us remark, that, living as we do in a day of abounding error, it solemnly behoves those who believe the truth, *fearlessly to maintain it*. Let there be no compromise, no barter of the truth; buy it at any sacrifice of human opinion, sell it at no price whatever. " Buy the truth, and sell it not." Stand up a witness of the truth, humbly, boldly, and in the strength of the Lord, wherever his providence may place you. O consider the honour of being permitted to testify to the truth as it is in Jesus! You may be a lone, a solitary witness, yet fear not; he who is " the truth " itself says to you, as he did to the church in Philadelphia,—" Thou hast a little strength, and hast kept my word, and hast not denied my name. Because thou hast kept the word of my patience, I also will keep thee from the hour of temptation, which shall come upon all the world, to try them that dwell upon the earth. Behold, I come quickly; hold that fast which thou hast, that no man take thy crown." Rev. iii. 10, 11.

Let those who hold the truth, *be careful to maintain good works, and so walk in all the holiness of the truth they profess*; let them see that by no carelessness of deportment, by no want of integrity, by no neglect of the means of grace, by no exhibitions of unholy temper, by no worldly conformity, yea, by no inconsistency whatever, they bring a slur upon the holy doctrines they avowedly maintain and love; let them not be satisfied with maintaining a string of doctrines, unaccompanied with their sanctifying power: but let them see that with the truth in their judgments, they possess grace in the heart, and unspotted holiness in the life. "Then said Jesus to those Jews which believed on him, If ye continue in my word, then are ye my disciples indeed; and ye shall know the truth, and the truth shall make you free." John viii 31, 32.

CHAPTER VI

ON GRIEVING THE SPIRIT

"Grieve not the Holy Spirit of God."—Eph. iv. 30.

THIS subject stands in close and solemn relation to the spiritual
and personal declension of the believer: his decay in grace
necessarily and painfully involves it. Of all that has been
wrought in the believer in the way of conviction, repentance,
faith, joy, holiness, &c., the blessed and Eternal Spirit is the
sole Author. Great and glorious is his work: yea, but for it,
the redemption accomplished by our Lord Jesus Christ, as to
any saving effects, would have availed nothing. The "Sun of
righteousness" might have risen upon the world in all his peer-
less splendour; but until the mental eye had been opened by
the Holy Spirit, not a beam had found its way into the dark
chambers of the understanding and the heart. The Gospel
"supper" might have been prepared, the Lamb slain, and the
invitation issued; but without a supernatural power working
upon the will, the desires, and the affections of man, all would
have "made light of it, and have gone their ways, one to his
farm, another to his merchandise." "It is expedient for you
that I go away," said Jesus, "for if I go not away, the Comforter will not come unto you; but if I depart, I will send him
unto you. And when he is come, he will reprove the world of
sin, and of righteousness, and of judgment." Our views of the
work of the Spirit cannot be too spiritual, nor can our estimate of its value be too high. The great danger to which we

are exposed, is, not in overrating, but in undervaluing the office-work of the Spirit; not in thinking too high, but in thinking too low of it: and that anything tends more to wound, grieve, and chase from us his sensible presence, than a known and permitted declension of his work, we cannot imagine. This is the solemn and important point, to which the consideration of the reader is now to be directed.

The phrases, "vexing the Spirit," "grieving the Spirit," "quenching the Spirit," "resisting the Spirit," &c., though metaphorical, are nevertheless highly significant and solemn in their meaning. Grief is not a passion in the Holy Spirit, as it is in us, any more than "anger," "wrath," "revenge," are unholy emotions in God, though ascribed to him. In condescension to our weakness, these expressions are employed to set forth God's extreme hatred of sin, and the holy sensitiveness of the Eternal Spirit to any neglect, undervaluing, or declension of his most gracious work and influence in the soul. Properly, the Spirit cannot be grieved, cannot be quenched, cannot be resisted; because he is not a creature, though a person. To believe the contrary, would be to invest the Holy Spirit of God with such attributes as would be incompatible with his Divine glory and infinite perfections,—such as belong only to a weak, sinful, finite creature. But, metaphorically, to "grieve the Spirit" is to disregard his voice, oppose his influence, and slight his kind, loving, and tender nature; and thus cause a withdrawment from the soul—in some cases temporary, in others eternal—of his presence, influence, and blessing. In the case of the regenerate, the withdrawment of the Spirit on being grieved, is for a season only; in that of the finally impenitent and unbelieving, the hushing of his voice, speaking to them in conscience, in providence, and in his word, is the giving of them up for ever. But these are points that will appear in a more advanced elucidation of our subject. Let our attention now be directed to the way in which the Holy Spirit

of God may be grieved, and then to the consideration of some
of the certain and mournful consequences.

I am supposed to address myself to those who admit, in its
unlimited meaning, the scriptural doctrine of the *Divine Personality* of the Holy Spirit: else it might be proper to show,
that a denial of this truth involves an absolute denial of the
Spirit,—his personal glory and official work,—and charges
home upon the conscience of the rejecter, a sin of the most
malignant character, and of the most fatal tendency. It surely
needs not the reasoning of a moment to prove that any existing doubt, any latent suspicion, as to the Spirit's right to
Divine homage, must involve the sin of grieving the Spirit in
the highest degree. Let the spiritual coldness, sterility, lethargy, which are the legitimate and certain results, prove the
truth of what we affirm. The moment a man entertains views
of the Spirit derogatory from his personal dignity, that moment he seems like one abandoned of the Spirit to the fearful
and ruinous consequences of his sin: his spirituality withers,
his grace decays, the spirit of devotion languishes, and at
length expires. If he ministers in the pastoral office, all power
and unction in his ministrations evaporate; or if he moves in a
private walk, all zeal, and ardour, and devotedness in the cause
of Christ become stagnant, and the curse and the reproach of
barrenness fall like a blight upon the once fertile and flourishing soul. These dire effects may be traced to low views of the
personal dignity and official work of the Holy Spirit. But I
now particularly address myself to those Christians who acknowledge the deity cf the Spirit, and his distinct personality
in the Godhead, and who humbly hope they are the subjects
of his renewing grace, and thus are acquainted with the power
and glory of his work. That even such may sadly grieve the
Holy Spirit of God, and in consequence be great spiritual
losers, we think the following considerations, deduced from
the inspired word, will clearly show.

We commence with that which bears most directly upon

the subject of the present volume, *the declension of the Spirit's work of grace in the soul of a child of God*. What can grieve the Spirit more than this? It is an awful slight cast upon the most glorious and stupendous production of his power: nowhere has he erected a temple so glorious, and nowhere has he put forth energy so mighty, and in nothing has he imprinted so deeply the outline of his own holy character, as in the work of grace which he has commenced, and carries on in the heart of man. Now, to witness any decay, declension, or languor in this work; to mark the loss of vigour, healthfulness, or fruitfulness, in any single grace; to see those whose souls he had quickened, whose minds he had illumined, whose affections he had detached from earthly things and centred in God, who did seem to "run well" and promised much fruit, and "an abundant entrance into the everlasting kingdom," now slacken their pace, grow weary of the way, fold their arms again in slumber, grow earthly, sensual, and grovelling; the temple neglected, its gates unwatched, and other guests admitted; holy motives losing their power, love ceasing to constrain, spiritual things no longer attracting, delighting, and satisfying the soul,—oh! can we imagine the loving, faithful, tender heart of the Spirit more sensibly touched with grief by anything than this? Well might he exclaim, "What could I have done more for my vineyard than I have done? Why, then, when I looked for grapes, did it bring forth wild grapes?" "O Ephraim, what shall I do unto thee? O Judah, what shall I do unto thee? for your goodness is as a morning cloud, and as the early dew it goeth away."

Of all spiritual states, *lukewarmness* is most abhorrent to God, and grieving to the Holy Spirit. "I know thy works, that thou art neither cold nor hot: I would thou wert cold or hot. So then because thou art *lukewarm*, and neither cold nor hot, I will spue thee out of my mouth." Thus has God declared his utter detestation of this state. And yet, who contemplates it in this awful light; who pauses to examine himself, to ascertain what real progress his soul is making,—what grace is enfeebled,—what part of the Spirit's work is decayed,—what spot of his soul is barren and unfruitful, and how far he is secretly and effectually grieving the Holy Spirit, by a known, allowed, and cherished state of spiritual declension? If, after all his skill, it must be affecting to the architect to witness the decay of his building; if so to the parent, after his costly expenditure of means in education, to witness the fond hopes he cherished of his child blasted, how infinitely more is the Spirit affected and grieved to behold the temple he has erected at such a cost, falling to decay; the soul he had taught with such care and solicitude, receding into a state of coldness and formality in its spiritual duties and affections! " The heart of the Spirit," beautifully remarks Dr. Owen, " is infinitely more tender towards us, than that of the most affectionate parent can be towards an only child. And when he with cost and care hath nourished and brought us up into some growth and progress in spiritual affections, wherein all his concerns in us do lie, for us to grow cold, dull, earthly-minded, to cleave unto the pleasures and lusts of this world, how is he grieved, how is he provoked!" See, then, that your spiritual state is such as occasions joy rather than grief to the Holy Spirit of God. Nothing can fill his loving heart with greater and more holy delight, than to witness the deepening character and expanding influence of his own work in the believer. To behold the glimmering light which he created, " shining more and more,"—the gentle plant emitting its fragrance and putting forth its fruit,—the well-spring in the heart rising heavenward, Godward,—such a picture must be grateful to the Spirit. If the enthroned Redeemer looks down with satisfaction upon the travail of his soul in the calling in of his redeemed, equally joyous must it be to the Eternal Spirit, to behold the widening of *his* kingdom in the saints,—the maturing of the soul for the inheritance and the companionship of " just men made perfect." To mark a growing conformity to the image of Christ—holiness expanding its root—each grace in active exercise—every weight cast aside—every sin mortified, and the whole body, soul, and spirit, a rising temple to God, must indeed fill all heaven with joy. Christian reader, see well to thy state, that the Holy Spirit of God is not grieved at any known and cherished declension of his work in thy soul.

The Spirit is grieved *by a denial, or undervaluing of his gracious work in the heart.* It is a circumstance worthy of remark, and important in the instruction which it conveys, that, among all the examples of deep humility, self-abasement, consciousness and confession of sin recorded of the saints in the word, not one appears to afford an instance of a *denial* or *undervaluing* of the Spirit's work in the heart. Keen as appears to have been the sense of unworthiness felt by Jacob, David, Job, Isaiah, Peter, Paul, and others; deep as was their conviction, and humiliating as were their confessions of sin's exceeding sinfulness, not one expression seems to betray a denial of the work of the Holy Ghost in their souls: they felt, and mourned, and wept, and confessed as men called of God, pardoned, justified, adopted, not as men who had never tasted that the Lord was gracious, and who therefore were utter strangers to the operation of the Spirit upon their hearts: they acknowledged their sinfulness and their backslidings as *converted* men, always ready and forward to crown the Spirit in his work. But what can grieve the tender, loving heart of the Spirit more deeply than *a denial of his work in the soul?* And yet there is a perpetual tendency to this, in the unbelieving doubts, legal fears, and gloomy forebodings which those saints yield to, who, at every discovery of the sin that dwelleth in them, resign themselves to the painful conviction, that they have been given over of God to believe a lie! To such we would earnestly say, Grieve not *thus* the Holy Spirit of God. Deep self-abasement, the consciousness of utter worthlessness, need not necessarily involve a denial of indwelling grace in the heart; yea, this blessed state is perfectly consistent with the most elevated hope of eternal life. He that can confess himself the "chief of sinners" and "the least of saints," is most likely to acknowledge, "I know in whom I have believed,"—"He hath loved me, and given himself for me." What! is it all fabulous that you have believed? is it all a delusion that you have experienced? have you been grasping at a shadow, believing a lie, and fighting as one that beateth the air? are you willing to yield your hope and cast away your confidence? What! have you *never* known the plague of your own heart, the *sweetness* of godly sorrow at the foot of the cross? have you *never* felt your heart beat one throb of love to Jesus? has his dear name *never* broken in sweet cadence on your ear? are you willing to admit that all the grief you have felt, and all the joy you have experienced, and all the blessed anticipations you have known, were but as a "cunningly devised fable," a device of the wicked one, a moral hallucination of the mind? O grieve not thus the Holy Spirit of God! deny not, undervalue not, his blessed work within thee! What if you have been led into deeper discoveries of your fallen nature, your unworthiness, vileness, insufficiency, declensions, and backsliding from God, we ask, Whose work is this? whose, but that same blessed, loving Spirit whom thus you are wounding, quenching, grieving, denying? On this point the writer feels acutely; when he remembers how many whose eye may trace this page, are in this very state,—not merely writing hard and bitter things against themselves, but also *against the blessed, loving, faithful Spirit of God,*—calling grace nature, denying his work in them, and, in a sense most painful to his tender heart, "speaking words against the Holy Ghost" he cannot but feel. There is much spurious humility among many saints of God, and this is one of its common forms. It is not *pride* gratefully to acknowledge what great things the Lord hath done for us,—it *is* pride that refuses to acknowledge them; it is not true *humility* to doubt, and underrate, until it becomes easy to *deny* altogether the work of the Holy Ghost within us,—it *is* true humility and lowliness to confess his work, bear testimony to his operation, and ascribe to him all the power, praise, and glory. See then, dear reader, that you cherish not this false humility, which is but another name for deep, unmortified *pride* of heart; remember that as Satan may transform himself into an angel of light, so may his agencies assume the disguise of the most holy and lovely graces; thus *pride*, one of his master agents of evil in the heart, may appear in the shape of the profoundest *humility*. And I would have you bear in mind, too, that though the work of the Spirit in your heart may, to your imperfect knowledge and dim eye, be feeble—the outline scarcely visible amid so much indwelling sin—the spark almost hid amid so much abounding corruption, yet, to the Spirit's eye, that work appears in all its distinctness and glory. "The Lord knoweth them that are his." This declaration will apply with equal truth to the knowledge which the Holy Ghost hath of his own work in the believer; his eye is upon the gentlest buddings of indwelling grace—the faintest spark of love—the softest whisper of holy desire—the most feeble yearnings of the heart towards Jesus,—all, all is known to, and loved by, the Spirit; it is his own work, and strange should he not recognise it. Suffer this consideration to have its proper weight in hushing those murmurings, and soothing those fears, and neutralising those doubts that so deeply grieve the Holy Spirit of God: yield yourself up unto him; humbly acknowledge what he has done in you; follow the little light he has given you, call into constant and active exercise the small degree of grace and faith which he has imparted, and seek " with all prayer and supplication " an enlarged degree of his holy, anointing, sanctifying, and sealing influence.

A substitution of his own work in the soul for the atoning and finished work of Jesus, greatly grieves the Holy Spirit of God. One essential and important office of the Spirit is to

glorify Christ: " He (the Spirit) shall glorify me," said Jesus;
" He shall testify of me "; " He shall take of mine, and shall
show it unto you." This being his work in reference to Christ,
it must be, of course, the great delight of the Spirit ever and
at all times to lift up Jesus and glorify him. And how does
the Spirit most glorify Christ, but by exalting his atoning
work,—giving to it the pre-eminence, the importance, and the
glory it demands,—leading the sinner, whom he has first convinced of sin, to accept of Jesus as a willing, an all-sufficient
Saviour,—to cast away all trust in self, all reliance upon a
covenant of works, which is but a covenant of death, and thus
going entirely out of himself, to take up his rest in the blood
and righteousness of Immanuel, the God-man Mediator. Oh,
what sweet, holy delight must it be to the Spirit of God, when
a poor sinner in all his conscious nothingness is led to build
upon Jesus, the " tried stone, the precious corner-stone, the
sure foundation!"

Let the reader, then, imagine how grieving it must be to the
Spirit, when there is any resting in *his* work in the soul, either
for acceptance, or for comfort, or for peace, or for strength,
or even for evidence of a state of grace, and not *solely* and
entirely in the atoning work which Jesus hath wrought out
for the redemption of sinners. The work of the Spirit and the
work of Christ, though they form parts of one glorious whole,
are yet *distinct*, and to be *distinguished* in the economy of
grace, and in the salvation of a sinner. It is the work of Jesus
alone, his perfect obedience to the broken law of God, and his
sacrificial death as a satisfaction of Divine justice, that form
the ground of a sinner's acceptance with God,—the source of
his pardon, justification, and peace. The work of the Spirit is,
not to atone, but to *reveal* the atonement; not to obey, but to
make known the obedience; not to pardon and justify, but to
bring the convinced, awakened, penitent soul to receive the
pardon and embrace the justification already provided in the
work of Jesus. Now, if there is any substitution of the Spirit's

work for Christ's work,—any undue, unauthorized leaning upon the work *within*, instead of the work *without*, the believer, there is a dishonour done to Christ, and a consequent grieving of the Holy Spirit of God. It cannot be pleasing to the Spirit to find himself a substitute for Christ; and yet this is the sin which so many are constantly falling into. If I look to convictions of sin within me, to any motion of the indwelling Spirit, to any part of his work, as the legitimate source of healing, of comfort, or of evidence, I turn my back upon Christ, I remove my eye from the cross, and slight his great atoning work; I make a Christ of the Spirit! I make a Saviour of the Holy Ghost! I convert his work into an *atoning* work, and draw the evidence and the consolation of my *pardon* and *acceptance* from what *he* has done, and not from what *Jesus* has done! O, is not this, again we ask, dishonouring to Christ, and grieving to the Holy Spirit of God? Think not that we undervalue the Spirit's work: great and precious is it. Viewed as a Quickener, John vi. 63—as an Indweller, 1 Cor. vi. 19—as a Sanctifier, 2 Thess. ii. 13—as a Sealer, Eph. i. 13—as a Witness, 1 John v. 10—as a Comforter, John xiv. 26—as the Author of Prayer, Rom. viii. 26,—his person cannot be too ardently loved, nor can his work be too highly prized: but the love we bear him, and the honour we give him, must not be at the expense of the honour and glory and love due to the Lord Jesus Christ, whom it is his office and his delight to glorify. The crown of *redemption* must be placed upon the head of Jesus; he alone is worthy to wear it,—he alone has a right to wear it. " *Thou* hast redeemed us by thy blood," is the song they sing in glory, and " *Thou* shalt wear the crown," should be the song echoed back from the redeemed on earth.

See, then, that you grieve not the Spirit, either by misplacing or by undervaluing the atoning work of Jesus. His blood, applied by the Spirit, pardons; his righteousness, received by faith, justifies you; and " the peace of God which passeth all understanding," is the certain and blessed fruit of both. The constant evidence of a pardoned and justified state, must spring from a constant dealing with, and looking to, the Lord Jesus; it is " in his light that we are to see light "; he is the Sun that shines upon the work within us. The eye of the soul withdrawn from his cross, and fixed in intense gaze upon itself, will soon be lost amid shadows and gloom. Inward joys may be lived upon, until the spring of joy ceases to flow; evidences may be looked to, until they melt away into darkness. What, under these circumstances, is the poor, distressed, alarmed soul to do, but to fly afresh to the cross? Where is it to look, but again unto Jesus? What is to speak a sense of pardon, but the atoning blood; and what is to assure of " perfect peace," but the justifying righteousness of the Son of God? O that there were a more simple and direct looking out of, and away from, self, to the atoning Saviour! Then would the precept be sweet, then would obedience be easy, then would the cross be light, and then, too, would peace flow as a river, and righteousness roll in as the waves of the sea.

And yet, there is a sense in which *the Spirit's own work may be so slighted*, as deeply to grieve his heart. There is a proneness to extreme points even in the child of God: he may either overrate, or he may underrate a thing; he may place an unwarrantable dependence upon that which, at another period, he may be found painfully and sinfully to slight. Thus, in reference to the afflictions of the believer, the word of God exhorts him on the one hand not to *despise* them, and tenderly admonishes him on the other hand not to *faint* under them. Heb. xii. 5. We may either think too much or too little of God's covenant chastenings. What need of the teachings of the Spirit every moment of one's life! how important to be found constantly distrusting and leaning off of self, and trusting to, and leaning upon Jesus! The prayer of a child of God should unceasingly be, that the Lord would keep him *from himself*; that the posture of his mind might be low at the feet of Jesus, each moment learning of, and living to him.

But how may the Spirit's work be slighted by the believer?
In various ways.

*He may cherish an imperfect consciousness of the indwell-
ing of the Spirit in his heart.* To show any indifference to the
presence of a guest, to manifest any want of marked and
proper attention, is a slight of no ordinary nature : in this
sense may the Holy Spirit of God be grieved. For the Holy
Ghost effectually to call, renew, sanctify, and take possession
of the soul—make it his temple, his permanent dwelling-
place; and yet, for that soul to entertain inadequate views of
this great truth, forget who is dwelling with and in him,
slight his heavenly guest, and go out and come in, and live
and act as if he were not a temple of the Holy Ghost,—what
can be more dishonouring to the Blessed and Eternal Spirit!
Oh that this momentous truth should even for a single moment be lost sight of by the believer! That he should be the
dwelling-place of the Most High, the 'High and Lofty One
that inhabiteth eternity, whose name is Holy,' the residence
of the Holy Ghost, and yet entertain a feeling or a thought
not in perfect harmony with so great a fact, does indeed show
the necessity of the apostolic admonition, 'Grieve not the
Holy Spirit of God.'

When, too, *his still small voice is unheeded, and his gentle
constraints are not yielded to*, there is a slight put upon his
work of a very grievous nature. The abiding Indweller of the
saint of God, the Spirit, is perpetually speaking to, admon-
ishing, leading, drawing, and constraining the soul; his great
work there is to teach, to sanctify, to shield, to check, and to
comfort the believer. Every holy shrinking from sin, every
firm resistance of its power, every victory achieved over its
motions, every aspiration after holiness, and every feeble desire to walk in the way of filial obedience to, and sweet communion with God, is the fruit of the indwelling Spirit in the
heart. How grieving, then, to that Spirit, when this loving
voice of his, and these gentle constraints of his, are over-

looked, stifled, disregarded, and slighted by the soul he so tenderly loves, and so faithfully watches over! Grieve not thus the Holy Spirit of God. In all his dealings with you, he seeks but your real good; he aims to deepen his own work in your hearts; he seeks but to promote your *holiness*, and to mature your soul for the joys and the companionship of the saints in light. Yet more; he desires your true *happiness*,—he would draw you off from carnal things, he would allure you from objects of sense and sin, and open to you springs of higher and purer enjoyment, and lead you into fairer and greener pastures: this would he do, by unfolding to you what you possess in Jesus, in the covenant of grace, and in a covenant God. Let your ear, then, be open to the gentle voice of the Spirit, and follow promptly and implicitly his secret and gentle leadings.

Inconsistency in the Christian profession must be highly grieving to the Holy Spirit of God. To mark a want of harmony between the professed principles and the habit of life in one avowedly his temple; to trace a love of the world, a panting for its fame, a grasping for its wealth, an adoption of its policy, a conforming to its maxims, its pursuits, its pleasures, and its religion, cannot fail to wound the sacred guest, the indwelling Spirit. And yet this worldly spirit, this painful inconsistency of avowed Christian principle, how many professors does it mark! What numbers there are professing and calling themselves Christians, the disciples of the Lord, the followers of the meek and lowly Lamb of God, who think lightly of putting on gay, worldly attire,—of frequenting balls, of moving in the dance, of joining in carnal music,—of attending plays, and reading novels and romances,—all of which are at variance with the Christian character, are violations of the Christian rule, are dishonouring to the name of Christ, and are deeply grieving to the Holy Spirit of God. You are professedly a temple to the Holy Ghost. What! shall you adorn that temple with earthly splendour, after the fashion

of this world? What says the Holy Ghost by his servant?—
" In like manner also, that women adorn themselves in modest
apparel, with shamefacedness and sobriety; not with broid-
ed hair, or gold, or pearls, or costly array; but (which becometh women professing godliness) with good works."
1 Tim. ii. 9, 10. Again,—" Whose adorning let it not be that
outward adorning of plaiting the hair, and of wearing of gold,
or of putting on of apparel; but let it be the hidden man of the
heart, in that which is not corruptible, even the ornament of
a meek and quiet spirit, which is in the sight of God of great
price. For after this manner in the old time the holy women
also, who trusted in God, adorned themselves." 1 Peter iii.
3-5. Do, then, the extravagance, the costliness, the worldliness, the studied attention to taste, that mark the outward
adornment of so many professing Christians, comport with
the spirit and the precept of the Gospel; rather, are they not
such indulgences as the Gospel clearly interdicts, and on
which Christianity severely frowns?

Again : Shall the believer, the professed temple of the Holy
Ghost, be found mingling with the world, taking pleasure in
its amusements, courting its society, working upon its principles, and adopting its policy? Ought this to be the line of
conduct pursued by a professing Christian? Is this the way
to illustrate the holy power of the truth, to recommend the
Gospel of Jesus Christ, to rebuke the sin, and folly, and rebel-
lion of the world, and to win it over to the obedience of the
faith? Assuredly not!

And how can the Divine life in the soul be fed and sustained from such a source? What nourishment does it derive
from the light and frothy readings of the day,—from the pages
of a sickly romance, a frivolous novel, a tale of fiction? What
food can the unhallowed, unsanctified imagination of men,
prepare for the strengthening, supporting, and expanding of
this Divine principle in the soul? Surely none.

And what a meetness for prayer, for communion with God,

for the reading of his sacred word, can a believer find in the giddy dance, in carnal song, in the immoral novel? What preparation of mind do these pursuits afford for approaching to God, for the proper discharge of Christian duties, for sober reflection, for the hour of death, and for the day of judgment? Oh! the awful inconsistencies that mark the profession of some, who can find a near and an easy path from the sanctuary, the communion table, and the closet, to the evening party, the ball-room, the mazy dance, the empty novel, the very *heart* of a gay and giddy world! Is this true Christianity? is this like Christ? is it after his command, his precept, and his example? Judge ye.

But what is the line of duty marked out for the walk of a professing believer? It is as clear in the word of God, as the meridian sun. Thus is it laid down: " Be not conformed to this world: but be ye transformed by the renewing of your mind, that ye may prove what is that good, and acceptable, and perfect will of God." Rom. xii. 2. " Come out from among them, and be ye separate, saith the Lord, and touch not the unclean thing; and I will receive you, and will be a Father unto you, and ye shall be my sons and daughters, saith the Lord Almighty." 2 Cor. vi. 17, 18. " Love not the world, neither the things that are in the world. If any man love the world, the love of the Father is not in him. For all that is in the world, the lust of the flesh, and the lust of the eye, and the pride of life, is not of the Father, but is of the world." 1 John ii. 15, 16. " Ye adulterers and adulteresses, know ye not that the friendship of the world is enmity with God? whosoever therefore will be a friend of the world, is the enemy of God." James iv. 4. " Pure religion and undefiled before God and the Father, is this—to visit the fatherless and widows in their affliction, and to keep himself unspotted from the world." i. 27. Thus implicitly and clearly is the line of Christian duty, in reference to a believer's connexion with the world, laid down by the Holy Ghost; he cannot depart from it without grieving the Spirit, wounding his own soul, and compromising his Christian profession.

Grieve not, then, the Holy Spirit of God by any known inconsistency of conduct, any sinful conformity to the world, any inordinate pursuit of its wealth, its honours, its pleasures, its friendships, and its great things. Pray against the sin of covetousness, that canker-worm that feeds at the root of so many souls; pray against a love of dress, that sin that diverts the mind of so many professors from the simplicity of Christ, and takes the eye off from the true adornment;—pray against a thirst for light and trifling reading, that strange and sinful inconsistency of so many, the certain tendency of which is, to starve the life of God in the soul, to engender a distaste for spiritual aliment, for the word of God, for holy meditation, and for Divine communion and fellowship;—yea, pray against the spirit of worldly, sinful conformity in *everything*, that the Holy Spirit be not grieved, and that Christ be not dishonoured and crucified afresh in and through you. It is to be feared that much of the professed Christianity of the day is of a *compromising* character. The spirit that marks so many is, " What will ye give me, and I will deliver him unto you?" There is a betraying of Christ before the world—a bartering of Christianity for its good opinion, its places of honour, and influence, and emolument. The world, the flesh, and Satan, are ever on the alert to frame a bargain with a Christian professor for his religion. " What will you give me in return?" is the eager inquiry of many. Oh, awful state! oh, fearful deception! oh, fatal delusion! Reader! are you a professing Christian? Then guard against the least compromise of your principles, the least betrayal of Jesus, the first step in an inconsistency of walk: above all, pray and watch against a *worldly Christianity*, a Christianity that wears a fair exterior, so far as it is composed of attendance upon sanctuary services, and sacraments, and religious institutions, but which excludes from it the cross of the meek and lowly Lamb of

God,—a Christianity which loves the world and the things of the world, "makes a fair show in the flesh," speaks well of Christ, and yet betrays him with a kiss.

But let not this be the model of *your* religion. You are not of the world, even as Christ was not of the world; if the world hate you, it hated him also before it hated you: if you were of the world, the world would love you. Marvel not at this! Do not expect more from the world than your Master received. The world that crowned your Lord with thorns, will never, if you "live godly in Christ Jesus," crown you with garlands: the world that crucified him, will never, if you are his consistent disciple, enthrone you. The world is the sworn *enemy* of your Saviour, let it not be *your friend*. No; come out of it, and be ye separate. Let your whole life be a solemn rebuke of it: let your integrity rebuke its want of principle,— your sobriety rebuke its frivolousness,—your upright sincerity rebuke its heartlessness,—your crucifixion to it rebuke its emptiness, folly, and sinfulness,—let your dress, your spirit, your whole conversation evince what a *splendid nothing* is all its pomp, and glory, and pretension: so shall you resemble your Lord and Master,—he who loved you unto the death, whose glory was in his humiliation, whose path was humble, lowly, and obscure, and whose death was the ignominious and accursed death of the cross: thus, too, you shall resemble his beloved apostle, who, taking his place by the cross, and looking down upon the world from the holy elevation where he stood, could exclaim, " God forbid that I should glory, save in the cross of our Lord Jesus Christ, by whom the world is crucified unto me, and I unto the world."

The Spirit may be grieved *by a slight put upon the means of grace*: these are his channels for the conveyance of his covenant blessings into the soul. He works not by miracles now, but by instrumentalities, by various agencies and means: he communicates his blessing and transmits his voice through the word, the ministry, the mercy-seat, and various other channels which he has graciously provided for the spiritual nourishment of the Divine life in the soul. Slight them not, undervalue them not, neglect them not. Look not for his blessing, nor expect to hear his voice, save as you are found walking in his own appointed way; you will grieve him, and cause him to withdraw his sensible presence, if any mean of grace is wilfully undervalued and neglected by you. These are the green pastures, where the shepherd causes his flock to rest at noon; these are the "still waters," where he leadeth their souls: and if the back is turned slightingly upon them, leanness and barrenness, coldness and death, must ensue. "They that wait upon the Lord shall renew their strength; they shall mount up with wings as eagles; they shall run and not be weary, and they shall walk and not faint."

In a word; the Spirit is grieved by any deviation from the strict and holy walk of a child of God—by any sense of guilt retained upon the conscience—any sin unconfessed, unrepented, and unforsaken—any known defilement of the temple he inhabits—any slight put upon Jesus—any neglect of the atoning blood—any light and trifling deportment—any uncharitable walk towards other Christians—any taking of the judgment-seat against them—all these must be grieving to the Holy Spirit of God.

CHAPTER VII

THE FRUITLESS AND THE FRUITFUL PROFESSOR

" Every branch in me that beareth not fruit he taketh away; and every branch that beareth fruit, he purgeth it, that it may bring forth more fruit."—John xv. 2.

IF there were any one feature in our Lord's ministrations more peculiarly impressive than another, it was the discriminating character that marked them. No one, on hearing him, could retire without the deep conviction that *he* was the man whose moral image Jesus had been drawing, and in such true and vivid resemblance, as to compel him to acknowledge the faithfulness of the portrait. There was no personality, no harshness, no unnecessary keenness in his reproof, no exaggeration of colouring, nothing overdrawn; but such a simple, faithful, scriptural dealing with human conscience, as either compelled his hearers to submit to his authority, and rank themselves among his followers, or to retire, silenced, self-accused, and self-condemned. Thus it is recorded at the conclusion of one of his discourses,—" And when the chief priests and Pharisees had heard his parables, they perceived that he spake of them." Matt. xxi. 45; and on another occasion we read, as the result of one of his peculiar and emphatic modes of teaching,—" And they which heard it, being convicted by their own conscience, went out one by one, beginning at the eldest, even unto the last." John viii. 9.

In the parable of the vine and the branch, we have, perhaps, one of the most striking specimens of our Lord's analytical style of instruction. He who formed the heart, and knew, in consequence of its apostasy, how deeply it was tainted with evil, was not ignorant how far a man could go in an outward profession of his name, and yet live and die destitute of regenerating grace. In the parable, therefore, to which we have alluded, he goes into a faithful and searching discrimination of character, lays bare the evil to which men were exposed, warns them of the danger of self-deception, distinguishes between the true and the false professor, and describes, in striking and affecting terms, the final state of both: "I am the true vine, and my Father is the husbandman. Every branch in me that beareth not fruit he taketh away: and every branch that beareth fruit, he purgeth it, that it may bring forth more fruit." In these words of our dear Lord, we have first, a solemn description of a fruitless professor; he then directs us to the pruning of the fruitful branch, and he assigns a reason why he prunes it—"that it may bring forth more fruit." Let us, in the present chapter, take the description of the *fruitless professor* as the basis of our first reflections.

That there can exist such a state as a *fruitless professor* of the Gospel, is, perhaps, one of the most indubitable evidences of the deep degeneracy of the human heart, and its natural tendency to self-deception, that exists. "The heart is deceitful above all things, and desperately wicked": and here is the proof, if all other were wanting, that an individual may approach so near in his external resemblance to a child of God, may look so like a believer in Jesus, may appear to be united to him, and still remain among the dead. Of all states this side of eternity, this is the most awful: and yet it is to be feared, if we are to judge of the tree by its *fruits*, and not by its *leaves*, that this is the state of thousands at the present moment. How important, may we not pause to remark, that the ministers of the Gospel—those who stand between the living and the dead—should model their ministry, as closely as they can, after their blessed Lord's; that they should be careful *how* they preach—that their preaching should be discriminating without being harsh, pointed without being personal, searching without being caustic; that no hearer should go away from beneath their ministrations, without a faithful delineation of his own character, the voice sounding in his conscience, and following him amid all his windings and his wanderings, " *Thou* art the man."

An expression of our Lord's may need a moment's explanation : he speaks of the fruitless branch as united to himself,— " Every branch *in me* that beareth not fruit." We are not to understand this of a vital union, a spiritual grafting into Christ; the analogy of truth is opposed to such an interpretation. The word of God invariably maintains the influential character of a living faith,—that it is ever productive of the fruits of holiness,—that a union to Christ will always result in a living to God : to suppose, therefore, that a dead and fruitless branch could be vitally in Christ, is to suppose that the word of God was against itself, which it can never be. But we are to understand our Lord as referring to an *external union*, to an *outward profession* only. There is such a thing as being externally in Christ; in him by an avowal of attachment to his cross, by a profession of his name, by adherence to his cause, by an apparent zeal for his glory : all this may exist, and in thousands does exist, without one particle of real, spiritual, life-deriving union to Christ. We may repair to a nursery, and may lop off a branch from a dead tree, and simply tie it to a living tree, and to all appearance it may resemble a true vital graft. A casual observer may be deceived; but time proves its false appearance : we come and look for fruit, the natural result of true grafting, and we find nothing save a lifeless, sapless, barren branch, externally united to the living tree. Look at such a professor! Where is the fruit? where is the real severing from the wild olive-tree? where is the great separation between himself and his own righteousness? where is the breaking up of the fallow ground of a hard, corrupt, stony heart? where is the humble, lowly, contrite spirit? where is the self-loathing, self-abhorrence, self-accusing, self-condemnation? Hear we the cry, " God be merciful to me a sinner?" Mark we the low posture in the dust, the smiting upon the breast, the standing afar off, the eye not lifted even towards the dwelling-place of a holy God? Where, too, is a living faith in Christ, a living upon Christ, and a living to Christ? Where is conformity to the Divine image? Where the fruits of holiness increasing and abounding? What of the spirit, the meekness, the lowliness, the gentleness, the sanctity of Jesus, do we discover? What self-denial, bearing of the cross, crucifixion to sin, deadness to the world, and living for eternity, do we trace? Alas! alas! we have mistaken the external profession for a vital, spiritual union to Christ! And is it any marvel, that when we came seeking fruit from such a branch, we should have found none?

But look at the profession of our day. If to put on the Lord Jesus by an outward avowal of his religion,—if to profess and call themselves Christians,—if to bow the knee at the mention of his name,—if to partake of the outward symbols of his body and his blood,—if to speak well of Jesus,—assent and consent to his doctrine, approve of his Gospel, follow his ministers, crowd his temple, contribute liberally to his cause,— if *these* constitute the sole and essential elements of real spiritual union to Christ, then may we not exclaim,—" The millennium has broken upon us in noontide splendour!" We speak of no single sect, we speak of all religious sects, for among all are to be found the lifeless, fruitless professor. Was it not so in the days of our Lord, and during the searching ministry of his apostles? Discriminating in his preaching as he was, and vigilant as they were in their oversight of the flock, false professors abounded in their time, and even rose to places of distinction in the church. Look at the case of Simon

Magus; he was but a *fruitless professor*; concerning whom it is recorded, that he had " neither part nor lot in the matter—that his heart was not right in the sight of God—that he was in the gall of bitterness, and in the bond of iniquity." Look at the case of Demas; he was but a *fruitless professor*. " Demas hath forsaken me," writes the apostle, " having loved this present world." And look at that eminent and awful instance of a mere external union to Christ—a fruitless profession of his name—Judas Iscariot; in reference to whom, Jesus prays to his Father, " those that thou gavest me I have kept, and none of them is lost, but the son of perdition." And to those whose union to himself was but external, and where life was fruitless, our Lord alludes in these solemn words, " Strive to enter in at the strait gate : for many, I say unto you, will seek to enter in, and shall not be able. When once the master of the house is risen up, and hath shut to the door, and ye begin to stand without, and to knock at the door, saying, Lord, Lord, open to us; and he shall answer and say unto you, I know you not whence ye are. Then shall ye begin to say, We have eaten and drunk in thy presence, and thou hast taught in our streets. But he shall say, I tell you, I know you not whence ye are; depart from me, all ye workers of iniquity. There shall be weeping and gnashing of teeth, when ye shall see Abraham, and Isaac, and Jacob, and all the prophets, in the kingdom of God, and you yourselves thrust out." Luke xiii. 24-28. If possible, in yet more awful terms does the word of God unfold the final doom of the Christless, fruitless professor. " Every tree which bringeth not forth good fruit, is hewn down and *cast into the fire*." " Whose fan is in his hand, and he will thoroughly purge his floor, and gather his wheat into his garner; *but he will burn up the chaff with unquenchable fire*." Matt. iii. 10, 12.

But it is not often the case that the fruitless professor clings even to his bare profession, until his doom arrives. There are many, who, long before the awful note of approaching judgment falls on their ear, throw off the outward garb, and stand forth in their true character. Our Lord seems to intimate this in various parts of his word; especially in his explanation of the parable of the sower, does he refer to it in clear and affecting terms,—" Those by the way side are they that hear; then cometh the devil, and taketh away the word out of their hearts, lest they should believe it and be saved. They on the rock are they, which, when they hear, receive the word with joy; and these have no root, which for a while believe, and in time of temptation fall away. And that which fell among thorns are they, which, when they have heard, go forth, and are choked with cares and riches and pleasures of this life, and bring no fruit to perfection." Luke viii. 12-14. These are they whom the spiritual Husbandman "taketh away." The season of temptation, the time of persecution, the accumulation of worldly cares, the increase and glitter of riches, are periods and occasions that place a man's religion in the crucible, that bring it to the test. The bare professor cannot stand it. The wind sweeps over the tree, and all its leaves are scattered. The fire kindles around the ore, and proves it to be base metal. But let us not be misunderstood. We dare not affirm of all mere profession of the Gospel, that its false character soon discovers itself. There are thousands who make mammon their trust, " whose god is their belly, whose glory is their shame, who mind earthly things"; and whose " end," if they are not brought to true repentance, will be " destruction": who yet, in the midst of it all, rigidly maintain the form of godliness, and who would regard it as the greatest offence, were their Christianity for a moment doubted. Oh, the heart is deep and treacherous as the sea; and they who trust it will be fearfully and eternally ruined! A man may be a lover of pleasure, and a lover of the world, and a lover of sin,—his heart may go after covetousness, and his mind may be immersed in worldly cares, and all the while be a rigid formalist, and a proud Pharisee, and a noisy disputant, and even suffer persecution for conscience' sake, rather than yield a principle bearing upon some lesser matter of the law. But we would now turn the reader's attention to THE PRUNING OF THE FRUITFUL BRANCH.

Our dear Lord's words are deep and rich in meaning: "Every branch that beareth fruit, he purgeth it." Here is life, here is true union; it is a fruitful branch, deriving its fruitfulness from its vital union to the Lord Jesus Christ. It will be observed, that this fruit-bearing branch is *in Christ*; grafted upon him, united to him, and dwelling in him, as the branch is *one* with the vine. The union of the believer with Jesus, and the consequent fruitfulness, is a glorious truth: the Holy Ghost, in his word, has laid great stress upon it. It is spoken of as a being *in Christ*: "Every branch *in me*"; "If any man be *in Christ*, he is a new creature"; "So we, being many, are one body *in Christ*"; "They that are fallen asleep *in Christ*." But in what sense are we to understand this being "in Christ"? We have shown how a fruitless professor may be externally united to Christ, there being no Divine life in the soul, no true faith, and consequently no spiritual fruitfulness: he is "dead while he liveth." But to be in Christ truly, spiritually, vitally, is more than this; it is to be in that eternal covenant of grace made with Christ, as the Surety and Mediator of his people; one of the number spoken of as the Lord's "peculiar treasure,"—"For the Lord hath chosen Jacob unto himself, and Israel for his peculiar treasure," Psalm cxxxv. 4; and concerning whom the Holy Ghost declares that they are *elected in Christ*,—"Blessed be the God and Father of our Lord Jesus Christ, who hath blessed us with all spiritual blessings in heavenly things in Christ: according as he hath *chosen us in him* before the foundation of the world, that we should be holy and without blame before him in love." Eph. i. 3, 4. To be "in Christ" truly, is to stand accepted in his righteousness, to be justified by him freely from all things; it is to be brought to the knowledge of our own vileness, insufficiency, and guilt; to be made to cast aside all self-dependence, that is, all works of human merit, and to come as the thief on the cross came, without any allowed confidence in aught of self, but as a poor, helpless, ruined, condemned sinner, all whose hope of pardon and acceptance is through the free mercy of God in Christ Jesus. To be " in Christ," is to be the subject of a living, holy, influential principle of faith; it is to be brought into the blessed state thus described by the apostle as his own : " I am crucified with Christ : nevertheless I live; yet not I, but Christ liveth in me; and the life which I now live in the flesh I live by the faith of the Son of God, who loved me, and gave himself for me." Gal. ii. 20. To be " in Christ," is to be one with him; it is to be a member of his mystical body, of which he is the spiritual head; and the head and the members are *one*. It is to have Christ dwelling in the heart : " *Christ in you* the hope of glory "—" Know ye not that *Christ dwelleth in you*, except ye be reprobates?"—" I in them." Yea, it is to dwell in the *heart* of Christ; it is to rest there in the very pavilion of his love, to dwell there every moment, to be sheltered there from all evil, and to be soothed there under all sorrow. Oh blessed state of being " in Christ!" Who would not experience it? who would not enjoy it? " There is therefore now no condemnation to them that are in *Christ Jesus*, who walk not after the flesh, but after the Spirit." Rom. viii. 1.

These are the living branches, united to the true Vine, which bear fruit. From their union to the living Vine their fruit comes : " From me is thy fruit found "; " As the branch cannot bear fruit of itself, except it abide in the vine, no more can ye, except ye abide in me." And oh what precious fruit does such a living branch bear! the broken heart—the contrite spirit—the mourning over sin—the low, abasing, humbling views of self—the venturing by faith on a full, mighty, willing Saviour—the going out of self, and resting in his all-atoning work and all-satisfying righteousness. This is followed by a progressive advance in all holiness and godliness, the fruits of faith which are by Jesus Christ, abounding in the life, and proving the reality of the wondrous change,—the close walk with God,—the submission of the will in all things to his,—the conformity of the life to the example of Jesus,—the "power of his resurrection" felt—the "fellowship of his sufferings" known—and "conformity to his death" marking the entire man. Phil. iii. 10.

These are some of the fruits of a truly regenerate soul. The Holy Ghost testifies, that the "fruit of the Spirit is in all goodness, and righteousness, and truth"; and still more minutely as consisting of "love, joy, peace, long-suffering, gentleness, goodness, faith, meekness, temperance."

Now observe, it is the *fruitful branch* only that the Husbandman pruneth: "every branch that beareth fruit, he purgeth it." If it be asked—why? the answer is, because it is only the *fruitful* branch that beareth the pruning. He pruneth it, *because* it is fruitful, *because* it has life from, and union with, the Vine. This purging, or pruning of the fruitful believer by the Lord, *is the trial of his own work*. The very discipline which a covenant God employs with his child, proves the existence and reality of grace in the soul. It is not the lifeless branch that he pruneth, it is not the spurious ore that he putteth in the furnace. When he takes his child in hand to deal with him, it is with a view of drawing forth the grace which he has first implanted in the soul. The very trial of faith supposes the existence of faith; and the trial of any one grace of the Spirit, supposes the previous indwelling of that grace in the believer. No man goes to a dry well to draw water from it; no man goes to a bank in which he has made no previous deposit, to draw money from it. When God,— the spiritual Husbandman of the church,—comes into his garden, and walks amid the "trees of righteousness," and in his sovereignty marks one here and another there for discipline, for pruning, whom does he select for this blessed purpose, but the trees which he has himself planted? Jesus, the Vine, has declared, that "every plant which his heavenly Father hath not planted, shall be rooted up." And have we not often seen the solemn fulfilment of this threatening in the case of graceless professors?—the first blast of temptation has carried them away, root and branch. God, perhaps, has brought them into deep trial; the storm of adversity has fallen upon them; death has snatched away the " desire of their eyes with a stroke"; riches have taken wings and flown away; character has been assailed; temptations have overtaken them; and what has been their end? We look for their religion,—it has fled away like the chaff of the threshing-floor before the sweeping hurricane; their profession,—it is all gone; their prayers,—they have evaporated into empty air. The solemn "place of the holy" that knew them, knows them no more. And so it will prove with every plant that our heavenly Father has not planted; and so with all the wood, hay, and stubble, built upon an outward acknowledgment and profession of Christ. And oh their end! ' For if after they have escaped the pollutions of the world through the knowledge (not an experimental or saving knowledge is here meant) of the Lord and Saviour Jesus Christ, they are again entangled therein, and overcome, the latter end is worse with them than the beginning. For it had been better for them not to have known the way of righteousness, than, after they have known it, to turn from the holy commandment delivered unto them. But it is happened unto them according to the true proverb, " The dog is turned to his own vomit again; and the sow that was washed to her wallowing in the mire." ' 2 Pet. ii. 20-22.

But the true child of the covenant, the Lord tries; the living, fruitful branch, the Husbandman prunes. There is that in every believer, yea, the most eminent child of God,—eminent for his holy and close walk,—that needeth pruning. We cannot always see the *necessity* of the discipline; we wonder, often, why such a believer is so constantly, and, in a sense, so severely dealt with. We look at his godly conversation in all things; we mark his holy deportment, his consistent walk, his lowly spirit, his spiritual gifts and graces, his devotedness and zeal in the cause of the Lord, and we exclaim, "Lord, make me like him, as he is like thee!" And when we see the cedar in Lebanon bend before the sweeping tempest—when we mark how the man of God becomes the subject of the most overwhelming afflictions, how wave follows wave, and messenger after messenger comes with tidings of evil still more bitter than the last,—when we see this mercy blasted, that comfort removed,—here a check, and there a disappointment, and he whom we gazed upon as one in whom the Lord had deposited great grace, and favoured with peculiar nearness and conformity to himself, thus deeply afflicted,—we marvel that the dear Husbandman should prune him as he does. But what says the Husbandman?—"I, the Lord, search the heart." Here is the secret revealed; the *hidden evil* of that holy man of God we could not discover. The powerful corruptions that dwelt in his heart,—which he, in a degree, knew, and mourned over and confessed daily before the Lord,—were concealed from our eye; and while we were judging from outward appearance,—and, it may be, judging correctly too, for by their fruits we are to know the true and the false professors,—the Lord was probing and searching the heart, and for the subjugation of the evil that he discovered there, was thus disciplining, and pruning, and purging his beloved child.

Dear reader, if thou art experimentally acquainted with the truth as it is in Jesus, if thou art a living branch of the true Vine, it will be nothing new for you to be informed, that the Canaanites still dwell in the land. You will recollect, that when the children of Israel took possession of Canaan, although they conquered its inhabitants, and took supreme possession and government of the country, yet the former occupants of the soil they could not entirely dispossess. The circumstance is thus recorded: "The children of Manasseh could not drive out the inhabitants of those cities; but the Canaanites would dwell in that land." Josh xvii. 12. Now what these Canaanites, these heathenish idolators, were to the children of Israel, the *natural corruptions* of the heart are to the called children of God. After all that Divine and sovereign mercy has done for the soul,—though the inhabitants of the land have been conquered, and the heart has yielded to the power of omnipotent grace, and the "strong man armed" has been deposed, and Jesus has taken the throne,—yet the Canaanites will dwell in the land, and we cannot expel them thence. These are the natural corruptions of our fallen nature, the evils of a heart that is but partially renewed, the heathenish lusts, and passions, and infirmities that formerly were the sole occupants of the soil, and still dwell there, and which we shall never, in the present state, entirely dispossess. But what did the children of Israel do to these Canaanites, whom they could not drive out of the cities, but who would dwell in the land? We read in the 13th verse: "Yet it came to pass, when the children of Israel were waxing strong, that *they put the Canaanites to tribute*: but did not utterly drive them out." Now this is what the children of God must do with the spiritual Canaanites that yet dwell in the renewed heart: they cannot be driven out, *but they may be put to tribute*; they cannot be entirely extirpated, yet they may be brought into complete subjection, and even made to contribute to the spiritual advance of the soul, and to the glory of God. Yes, even these very indwelling and powerful Canaanites, these strong corruptions that war and fight in the renewed soul, may be made subservient to the spiritual benefit of a child of God. Will it not be so, if they lead him to put no confidence in himself, to draw largely from the fulness of grace in Jesus, to repair often to the throne of mercy, to deal much and closely with the atoning blood, to cultivate a watchful, prayerful, tender spirit and daily and hourly to rejoice in Christ Jesus, having no confidence in the flesh? And yet all this may be the result, when the believer has waxen strong in the Divine life, and has learned to put his indwelling corruptions to tribute, though he may not utterly expel them from his breast. Thus "God turned the curse of Balaam into a blessing," Neh. xiii. 2; and thus, too, may the renewed soul, —often led to exclaim, "O wretched man that I am? who shall deliver me from the body of this death?"—through a supply of the Spirit of Christ Jesus, and becoming more thoroughly versed in the art of the holy war, be able to turn the risings of his indwelling sins into occasions of more holy and humble walk with God. Happy believer, the tendency and real effect of whose indwelling infirmities of the flesh and the spirit are, to school the soul in the knowledge of its own nothingness, to constrain it to a soft and lowly walk, and to endear the blood, the mercy-seat, and the holy of holies, into which the most burdened, distressed, and humble soul may at all times enter!

This pruning does not destroy or weaken the power of the Divine life in the soul. We may go to a tree of the forest, and prune it of every branch, yea, we may level it to the earth; and yet,—the principle of life still remaining,—the genial showers, and the warm sunshine, will cause it again to spring forth and bud, blossom and bear fruit. The Divine life in the soul of man is indestructible,—it cannot perish; the seed that grace has implanted in the heart is incorruptible,—it cannot be corrupted. So far from trials, and conflicts, and storms, and tempests, impairing the principle of holiness in the soul, they do but deepen and strengthen it, and tend greatly to its growth. We look at Job; who of mere man was ever more keenly tried, or more closely pruned than he?— and yet, so far from destroying, or even weakening, the Divine life within him, the severe discipline of the covenant through which he passed, did but deepen and expand the root, bringing forth in richer clusters the blessed fruits of holiness. Think you, dear reader, the Divine life in his soul had undergone any change for the worse, when, as the result of God's covenant dealings with him, as the effects of the severe pruning of the fruitful branch, he exclaimed,—" I have heard of thee by the hearing of the ear, but now mine eye seeth thee: wherefore I abhor myself, and repent in dust and ashes?" No: the pruning of the fruitful branch impairs not, but rather strengthens and renders more fruitful the principle of holiness in the soul, as we now proceed to show. The pruning of the fruitful branch, our Lord declares, is with the view of its *increased fruitfulness*; " Every branch that beareth fruit, he purgeth it, *that it may bring forth more fruit.*"

It is the will of God that his people should be a fruitful people. " This is the will of God, even your sanctification,"— the sanctification of a believer including all fruitfulness. He will bring out his own work in the heart of his child; he will show that where grace dwells, it is productive of good fruit: and never does he take his child in hand with a view of dealing with him according to the tenor of the covenant of grace, but that dealing results in a greater degree of spiritual fruitfulness. Now, when the Lord afflicts, and the Holy Ghost sanctifies the affliction of the believer, are not these among the costly fruit of that discipline? In the first place, *self has become more hateful*. This, God declared, should be the result of his dealings with his ancient people Israel, for their idolatry,—" They shall loathe themselves for the evils which they have committed in all their abominations." And again,— " Then shall ye remember your ways, and all your doings wherein ye have been defiled: and ye shall loathe yourselves in your own sight, for all your evils that ye have committed." And when the Divine compassion was drawn forth, this is described as having been the state of his beloved people, —" None eye pitied thee, to do any of these unto thee, to have compassion upon thee; but thou wast cast out in the open field to the loathing of thy person." And this is no small fruit, the result of God's covenant dealings with the soul: it is one of the useless branches which he prunes away. To loathe self on account of its sinfulness, to mortify it in all its forms, and to bring it entirely into subjection to the Spirit of holiness, is indeed no small triumph of Divine grace in the soul, and no mean effect of the sanctified use of the Lord's dispensations. That must ever be considered a costly mean that accomplishes this blessed end. This unmortified *self* in the believer, is one of the most deadly enemies of his soul; it shows itself in a thousand ways, and wearing a thousand disguises. It is often difficult to detect the under-current working of the principle; for, frequently, where suspicion of its existence is most lulled to rest, *there* is it most rife and powerful. Self-confidence as in Peter, self-boasting as in Hezekiah, self-righteousness as in Job, self-deception as in Balaam,—in how many numberless ways may this hateful, ruinous principle discover itself! and how much " deceivableness of unrighteousness " is in it—is only fully known to him who solemnly declares, " I, the Lord, search the heart." Beloved reader, in thy heart and in mine, the principle of this sin exists; and who can search it out, and root it out, but the Lord the Spirit? " If we through the Spirit mortify the deeds of the body, we shall live." Is thy covenant God and Father dealing with thee now?. Pray that this may be one blessed result, *the abasement of self within thee*, the discovering of it to thee in all its modifications and deformity, and its entire subjection to the cross of Jesus. Blessed pruning, if the tendency and the effect are, to lay thee in the dust before the Lord, to cause thee to loathe thyself, and to go softly and lowlily all thy days!

Another holy tendency of the pruning of the fruitful branch, is, *to endear the Lord Jesus in his person, work, and offices*. Jesus, the " Branch," the " Plant of Renown," grows only upon the living and the pruned heart. There are many professors in whose hearts there is not room for Christ: the world, unmortified sin, take up all the space, occupy all the affections; and while his name is outwardly professed, His cross is inwardly despised. Oh, what emptying, what humbling, what pruning, are necessary, in order to make room for the lowly Lamb of God in the heart of a poor believing sinner! And for years after the first reception of Jesus, is this emptying and pruning needed. If it were not so, would our dear Lord discipline as he does? Would he sever this and that limb; would he cut off this and that dependence; would he take us off of creature trust, and that sometimes in the most painful way? Oh no! by these means he seeks to establish *himself* in our affections,—*he* would have our whole hearts, *he* would make us fruitful. And when thus unhinged from earthly trust, when emptied of confidence in self, when pruned of earthly comforts,—oh how unutterably precious does Jesus become! Then do we see him to be just the Jesus that we want, just the Saviour that we need: we find in him all that we ever found in the creature, and infinitely more— wisdom, strength, tenderness, and sympathy, surpassing all that men or angels ever felt, or could possibly feel, for us. Then it is, his blood and righteousness are endeared; then we fly to his fulness of all grace; and then the tender, bleeding branch takes a firmer hold on its stem, and henceforth looks only to it for all its vigour, its nourishment, and its fruit. " As the branch cannot bear fruit of itself, except it abide in the vine, no more can ye, except ye abide in me." Ah! beloved reader, if thou art his child, he will cause thee to know it, and will endear himself to thee as such. And this is seldom done, save in the way of severe pruning. Shrink not from it, then. All the good that the Lord ever takes from thee, he returns ten thousand-fold more *in giving himself*. If thou canst say, " the Lord is my portion," then what more dost thou, canst thou want? And remember, too, the Lord will prune thee of nothing that was for thy real good. He is the

Judge of what is best for thee, not thyself: he will sever the useless tendrils only, the small branches that consume the sap, that absorb the nourishment, and are productive of unfruitfulness. We are but imperfect judges of what tends best to our spiritual or temporal benefit. That which we may deem absolutely essential to both, the Lord in his wisdom and love may see proper to remove; and as frequently, that for the *removal* of which we had often besought the Lord, he may see fit to *retain*. Thrice Paul prayed for the removal of his infirmity, and thrice the Lord denied his request: but the denial was accompanied by a promise, calculated to soothe into sweet acquiescence every feeling of the apostle—" My grace," said the Lord, " is sufficient for thee." Let it ever be remembered by the tried believer, that *supporting grace, in the season of trial, is a greater mercy than the removal of the trial itself*. The Lord Jesus did seem to say to his servant, " I see not that it would be for thy good to grant thy prayer, but I will enable thee to bear the infirmity without a murmur: I will so support thee, so manifest my strength in thy weakness, my all-sufficiency in thy nothingness, that thou shalt not desire its removal." " Lord," he might have replied, " this is all that I desire. If thou in thy wisdom and love dost see fit still to prune me, I am in thy hands to do with me as seemeth good in thy sight. The continuance of the trial will but prove the strength of thy grace, and the tenderness and sympathy of thy heart." After this, we hear no more of Paul's thorn in the flesh: the grace of his Lord, doubtless, proved all-sufficient for him.

There are one or two points of *caution* and *encouragement* upon which we would touch before closing the chapter.

Let the believer beware, how he despises what little fruitfulness the Lord the Spirit may have given him: there is danger of this. Many who read this chapter, may close it with deep mourning over their barrenness; they may think their fruit nothing but leaves, their religion nothing but profession.

But stay, dear reader: it is a mercy for thee to know that the Lord does not regard *thy* estimate of a fruitful state; else, were the Lord to judge and condemn us as we do ourselves, were he to despise his own work as we too frequently do, it would indeed go hard with us. But he does not: that which we have often thought unworthy of his notice, he has looked down upon with the fondest complacency and delight. And when at the close of a sermon, or the reading of a book, or on retiring from the throne of grace, we have hung our heads, and blushed to lift our faces towards him, exclaiming,— "Lord, I am vile; look not on me, for I am black," he has beheld the fruit of his own Spirit, costly, fragrant, and precious in his sight. See, then, that you despise not what the Lord has wrought for you. Any desire of the heart for Christ, any secret brokenness, any godly sorrow over indwelling sin, any feeble going out of self and leaning on Jesus, is the gracious work of the Holy Ghost in the soul, and must not be undervalued or unacknowledged. A truly humble view of self, is one of the most precious fruits of the Spirit: it indicates more real fruitfulness, perhaps, than any other state of mind. That ear of corn which is the most full of grain, hangs the lowest; that bough which is the most heavily laden with fruit, bends the nearest to the ground. It is no unequivocal mark of great spiritual fruitfulness in a believer, when tenderness of conscience, contrition of spirit, low thoughts of self, and high thoughts of Jesus, mark the state of his soul. "Who hath despised the day of small things?"— not Jesus.

But, dear reader, rest not here; blessed as it is to know thy barrenness, and to mourn over it, it is still more blessed to press forward towards a deeper and more spiritual acquaintance with Christ, the source of all real fruitfulness. Too many rest in a mere deploring of their barrenness; they will ingenuously acknowledge their state, freely confess it before God, and yet meet them when you will, this is always their posture, and this their confession. One seems to mark in them no advance, no striving after higher attainments, the crucifixion of known infirmities, the mortification of easy besetting sins, the surrender of that which feedeth as a worm upon the root of their religion. There seems just life and consciousness enough to detect the secret declension of the soul, but not enough to arrest its progress.

But, reader, that this should not be thy case, *seek an increasing knowledge of Christ*; be assured of this,—here lies the grand secret of a growing, fruit-bearing Christian. " As the branch cannot bear fruit *of itself*, except it abide in the vine; no more can ye, except ye abide in me." There is a perpetual proneness to seek our fruitfulness from anything save a close, spiritual, and constant dealing with the cross of Jesus: but as well might we expect the earth to clothe itself with verdure, or the tree to blossom, and the blossom ripen into fruit, without the sun's genial warmth, as to look for fruitfulness in a regenerate soul, without a constant dealing with the Lord Jesus Christ; for, just what the sun is to the kingdom of nature, Jesus the Sun of righteousness is to the kingdom of grace,—the blessed source of all its verdure, fragrance, and fruitfulness. Then, let all your expectations be centred *here*. No real good can come to thee, no healing to thy spirit, no fruitfulness to thy soul, from a perpetual living upon convictions of sin, legal fears, or transient joys: the Divine life can derive no aliment from *these*. But live upon the atoning blood of Jesus. Here is the fatness of thy soul found; this it is that heals the wound, wins the heart, and hushes to repose every fear of condemnation; this it is that enables a poor sinner to look full at God, feeling that justice, holiness, truth, and every Divine perfection are on his side. It is the blood of Jesus, applied by the Spirit, that moistens each fibre of the root of holiness in the soul, and is productive of its fruitfulness; this it is that sends the warm current of life through every part of the regenerate man, quickening the pulse of love, and imparting a healthy and vigorous power to every act of obedience. And when the spiritual seasons change,—for it is not always spring-time with the soul of a child of God,—when the summer's sun withers, or the autumnal blast scatters the leaves, and winter's fiercer storm beats upon the smitten bough, the blood and righteousness of Christ, lived upon, loved, and cherished, will yet sustain the Divine life in the soul, and in due season the spring blossom and the summer fruit shall again appear, proving that the Divine life of a believer is " hid with Christ in God." Then shall it be said of you, as was said of the church by her Beloved: " The winter is past, and the rain is over and gone; the flowers appear on the earth, the time of the singing of birds is come, and the voice of the turtle is heard in our land. The fig-tree putteth forth her green figs, and the vines with the tender grape give a good smell. Arise, my love, my fair one, and come away." Sol. Song ii. 11-13. Then let your heart respond, " Awake, O north wind, and come, thou south, blow upon my garden, that the spices thereof may flow out." Thus shall you be " filled with the fruits of righteousness, *which are by Jesus Christ*, unto the glory and praise of God."

Afflicted believer, forget not that it is the *fruitful* branch only that the Lord pruneth: " Whom the Lord *loveth*, he chasteneth ": and again, he declares, " Whom I *love*, I rebuke and chasten." Then, thank him for the pruning; bless him for the sanctified trial that weans thee from earthly things, that deadens thy heart to every rival of Christ, and that imparts an upward spring to faith, hope, and love. Not one unkind thought is there in the heart of the God that now chastens you. True, he may have severed from thee branch after branch, he may cut off all thy earthly springs, he may lead thee down into the deep valley of abasement; yet still is he *love*, and nothing but love. Could you look into his heart,— not a spring would be found dwelling, nor a pulse beating there that would not speak of love to thee at this very moment. All that he seeks with regard to yourself, is your increased fruitfulness; and to promote your real *sanctification*, is to promote your real *happiness*. In all God's dealings with his covenant people, he seeks their greatest good, their highest happiness, and in nothing more manifestly than in this does he show the intense love which dwells in his heart towards them.

Frequently call to mind our Lord's words: "Herein is my Father glorified, that ye bear much fruit, so shall ye be (manifestly) my disciples." This "much fruit" is often found mostly in those with whom the Lord mostly deals. He has created his people for his own glory, and this he will secure to himself in their abundant fruitfulness. This is why the most illustrious saints have ever been the most deeply tried, severely pruned: their great fruitfulness sprang from their great afflictions. And yet, beloved, the Lord deals with his saints according to his holy sovereignty; not by one line, or in one path, does he always conduct them. Is God smiling upon thee? does the summer sun shine? is thy sea smooth and flowing? does the "south wind" blow upon thee? See, then, that thou walk humbly with God; "Be not high-minded, but fear." If God in his providence has elevated thee a little in the world, ye have need to besiege his throne for great grace to keep thy spirit *low* in the dust before him. Do thy fellows admire thy talents, extol thy gifts, applaud thy works, and court thy society? Oh how closely and softly and humbly ought you *now* to walk with God! That breath of adulation that lighted upon thee, will prove a blight upon thy graces, if thou go not upon thy knees before God; that flattering word which fell upon thine ear, will prove as the fly in the apothecary's ointment to thy soul, if thou get not closer down at the foot of the cross. Let every circumstance and state take thee there; whether the north wind or the south wind blows, whether the dark cloud of adversity gathers over thee, or the sunshine of prosperity beams upon thee—still let thy posture ever be low before the Saviour's cross; nothing can harm thee *there*. See that the season of outward prosperity is the season of thy soul's fruitfulness; see that every mercy takes thee to God; convert every new blessing into a fresh motive for living not unto thyself, but unto Him from whom the blessing came.

And if you are constrained to take your worst frames to Christ, your sins as they rise, your weakness as you are conscious of it, your corruptions as they discover themselves, even so shalt thou be a fruitful branch of the true Vine. In the very act of going, just as he is, to Christ, the believer brings forth fruit. For what marks the frame of the soul thus travelling up to the cross, but self-distrust, self-abasement, deep conceptions of its own nothingness, high views of Christ's sufficiency? And is not *this* precious and costly fruit? I know of none more so.

And let the fruitful believer anticipate the approaching period of his translation to a more genial and healthy soil. In heaven, the home of the saints, there will be nothing to blight the flower of grace; no frosts of winter, no burning heat of summer, no crushing storms, no sweeping tempests; the former things will all have passed away, and a new heaven and a new earth, in which dwelleth righteousness, shall have succeeded them. Happy hour of this release! *Here* he is a " lily among thorns"; *there* he will be a tree of righteousness, on which the storm will never rise, on which the sun will never set.

> " Oh what a garden will be seen,
>   When all the flowers of grace
> Appear in everlasting green,
>   Before the Planter's face!
>
> " No more exposed to burning skies,
>   Or winter's piercing cold;
> What never-dying sweet will rise
>   From every op'ning fold!

" No want of sun or showers above,
   To make the flowers decline;
Fountains of life and beams of love,
   For ever spring and shine.

" No more they need the quick'ning air,
   Or gently rising dew !
Unspeakable their beauties are,
   And yet for ever new.

" Christ is their shade, and Christ their sun;
   Among them walks the King :
Whose presence is *eternal noon,*
   His smile *eternal spring.*"

CHAPTER VIII

THE LORD, THE RESTORER OF HIS PEOPLE

" He restoreth my soul."—Psalm xxiii. 3.

THROUGHOUT the discussion of our subject, we have endeavoured to keep distinctly and prominently before the mind of the reader, the indestructible nature of the Divine life in the soul, the stability of the covenant of grace, and the unchangeableness of God's love towards his people. The proper unfolding of our theme demanded more than a bare recognition of these glorious Gospel truths: apart from them, upon what an uncertain tenure would the final salvation of the believer rest! When we are led to consider the uncertainty of the creature, —when we take the history of a child of God, compressed within the short period of a single day,—mark what flaws, what imperfections, what fickleness, what startings aside, what dereliction in principle, what flaws in practice, what errors in judgment, and what wanderings of heart, make up that brief history,—how are we led to thank God for the stability of the covenant! that covenant which provides for the full redemption of all believers,—which from eternity secures the effectual calling, the perfect keeping, and the certain salvation of every chosen vessel of mercy. With what distinctness and sweetness is this truth thus unfolded by God himself: " If his children forsake my law, and walk not in my judgments; if they break my statutes, and keep not my commandments; then will I visit their transgression with the rod, and their iniquity with stripes. Nevertheless, my loving-kindness will I not utterly take from him, nor suffer my faithfulness to fail: my covenant will I not break, nor alter the thing that is gone out of my lips." Psalm lxxxix. 30-34.

It will be seen, that two most solemn and affecting truths are recognised in this passage,—the backslidings of a child of the covenant, and the certainty of his restoration. It is more especially with the latter truth that we have to do in the present chapter.

Of the *necessity* that exists for the restorings of the Lord, we need not here say much, the preceding pages having gone at some length into this point; and yet it forms the basis of our present subject, and is too important to be dismissed with a simple allusion. That there exists a *necessity* for the Divine restorings, who can doubt, that remembers that *the Divine life of a believer has its residence in a heart but partially renewed and sanctified?* In the case of Adam before he fell, this was not so; there was nothing in his heart opposed to the life of God within him. The mind, the will, the affections, yea, the whole soul, were one glorious orb of perfect light and holiness: not a shadow dimmed its lustre, not a speck marred its beauty. Every faculty of the mind, every bias of the will, every emotion of the heart, every breathing of desire, were in agreement with its nature, and were favourable to its growth.

But not so is it now. Adam fell, and in his fall transmitted to his posterity a nature totally corrupt in every part; and although Divine and sovereign grace has undertaken to renew that nature, and does so in part, yet it is *but* in part renewed and restored to its original glory. The Divine life has its dwelling-place in a fallen, fleshly nature. One sentence of the apostle's explains and confirms this truth,—" The life which I now live in the flesh," Gal. ii. 20: the Divine life which he lived, was *in the flesh.* It was encompassed by all the corruptions, weaknesses, infirmities, and assaults of the flesh; there was not a moment that it was not exposed to assaults from within; there was not a natural faculty of the mind, or throb of the heart, that was favourable to its prosperity, but all were contrary to its nature, and hostile to its advance. Let every believer remember, that the Divine life which he lives, he lives *in the flesh*; and that there exists not a day that he stands not in need of the restorings of the Lord.

Connect with this the many *external* influences which are hostile to the Divine life in the soul. As there is nothing internal that is favourable to a state of grace, so there is nothing external that assists it forward. It has its many and violent enemies: Satan is ever on the watch to assault it,—the world is ever presenting itself in some new form of fascination and power to weaken it,—a thousand temptations are perpetually striving to ensnare it; thus its internal and external enemies are leagued against it. Is it, then, any wonder that faith should sometimes tremble, that grace should sometimes decline, and that the pulse of the Divine life should often beat faintly and feebly?

The saints in every age have felt and lamented this. Hence the prayer of David, which is the prayer of all true believers: " Hold thou me up, and I shall be safe "; implying the greatest weakness in himself, and his perpetual exposure to the greatest falls; " Hold thou me up, for only as I am upheld by thee, am I safe." Again he prays: " Keep back thy servant also from presumptuous sins; let them not have dominion over me "; implying that a believer left to the tendencies of his fallen nature, might become a prey to the worst sins: " Keep back thy servant also from *presumptuous* sins." In addressing himself to the converted Hebrews, the apostle seizes the occasion thus to exhort them: " Take heed, brethren, lest there be in any of you an evil heart of unbelief in departing from the living God." " In *departing*,"—implying a constant tendency to depart from God. And what does God himself say of his people? "My people are bent to backsliding from me." And again, "Why is this people of Jerusalem slidden back by a *perpetual* backsliding?" Yes, it is a perpetual proneness to declension. The sun rises but to set, the clock is wound up but to run down; and not more natural is it for them thus to obey the laws that govern them, than for the heart of a child of God to follow the promptings of its corrupt and wayward nature.

This leads us to touch upon the *principle* of all departure from God. We look at a believer's lax practice, we mourn and weep over it, and we do well; we trace our own, and still deeper shame and confusion of face cover us: but we forget that the cause of our bitterest sorrow and humiliation should be, the concealed *principle of evil* from whence springs this unholy practice. How few among the called of God, are found confessing and mourning over *the sin of their nature*— the impure fountain from whence flows the stream, the unmortified root from whence originates the branch, and from which both are fed and nourished! This is what God looks at,—the sin of our fallen, unsanctified nature,—and this is what we should look at, and mourn over. Indeed, true mortification of sin consists in a knowledge of our sinful nature, and its subjection to the power of Divine grace. The reason why so few believers "through the Spirit mortify the deeds of the body," is, a forgetfulness that the work has to do first and mainly with the *root* of sin in the soul: "Make the tree good, and the fruit will also be good"; purify the fountain, and the stream will be pure. Oh, were there a deeper acquaintance with the hidden iniquity of our fallen nature,—a more thorough learning out of the truth,—that "in our flesh there dwelleth no good thing,"—a more heartfelt humiliation on account of it, and more frequent confession of it before God,—how much higher than they now are would be the attainments in holiness of many believers!

There is, then, in every child of God, the innate *principle* of departure. Notwithstanding the wonders of grace God has wrought for the soul,—though he has elected, called, renewed, washed and clothed the believer; yet if he did not check and rein him in, he would depart, and that for ever!—this unsanctified, unmortified principle would bear him away. Is there not in this aspect of our theme something truly heart-breaking?—the subject of a kind and benevolent government, and yet to be always rebelling against the Sovereign; dwelling under a kind and loving Father's roof, and yet to be perpetually grieving him, and departing from him; to have received so many costly proofs of his love, and yet rendering the most ungrateful returns,—oh, it is enough to sink the soul in the deepest self-abasement before God! Reader, what has the Lord been to thee? Come, witness for him; has he ever been a wilderness to thee, a dry and barren land?—has there been aught in his dealings, in his conduct, in his way with thee, wherefore thou shouldst have turned thy back upon him?— has there been any harshness in his rebukes, any unkind severity in his corrections, anything judicial and vindictive in his dealings? Nay, on the contrary, has he not been a fruitful garden, a pleasant land, a fountain of living waters to thee? Has he not blended kindness with all his rebukes, tenderness with all his chastisements, love with all his dealings, and has not his gentleness made thee great? Then why hast thou departed from him? What is there in God that thou shouldst leave him, what in Jesus that thou shouldst wound him, what in the blessed Spirit that thou shouldst grieve him? Is not the cause of all thy departure, declension, unkindness, unfruitfulness, in *thyself*, and in thyself *alone*? But if this has been thy conduct towards God, not so has been his conduct towards thee. This brings us to the consideration of his *restoring* mercy.

The first point we would look at is, the *love* of the Lord Jesus in restoring a wandering believer. Nothing but the most infinite, tender, unchanging love, could prompt him to such an act. There is so much of black ingratitude, so much of deep turpitude in the sin of a believer's departure from the Lord, that but for the nature of Christ's love, there could be no possible hope of his return. Now this costly love of Christ is principally seen in his taking the *first step* in the restoring of the soul: the *first advance* is on the part of the Lord. This is too important a truth to be lightly touched upon. There is no more self-recovery after, than there is before, conversion; it is entirely the Lord's work. The same state of mind, the same principle that led to the first step in declension from God, leads on to each successive one: until, but for restraining and restoring grace, the soul would take an everlasting farewell of God. But mark the expression of David,— "He restoreth my soul." Who? He of whom he speaks in the first verse as his Shepherd,—"The Lord is my Shepherd." It is the *Shepherd* that takes the first step in the recovery of the wandering sheep. If there is one aspect in the view of this subject more touching than another, it is this,—that such should be the tender, unchanging love of Jesus towards his wandering child, he should take the first step in restoring him. Shall an offended, insulted Sovereign make the first move towards conciliating a rebellious people?—that Sovereign is Jesus: shall an outraged Father seek his wandering child, and restore him to his affections and his house?—that Father is God. Oh what love is that which leads Jesus in search of his wandering child: love that will not let him quite depart: love that yearns after him, and seeks after him, and follows after him through all his devious way, his intricate wanderings, and far-off departures; love that no unkindness has been able to cool, no forgetfulness has been able to weaken, no distance has been able to destroy!

Not less conspicuous is the *power* of Jesus in the restoring of the soul: "*He* restoreth my soul,"—he, the Omnipotent Shepherd. We want Omnipotence to bring us back when we have wandered; nothing less can accomplish it. We want the same power that converted, to re-convert; the power that created, to re-create us. This power Jesus possesses. It was essential to the full salvation of his church that he should have it; therefore, when praying to his Father, he says, " As thou hast given him power over all flesh,"—why this power? —" that he should give eternal life to as many as thou hast given him." It was necessary that he should have power over *all flesh*, yea, over all the powers leagued against the church, that he should bring to glory all that were given to him in the covenant of grace.

Now this power is gloriously exerted in the restoring of the soul. Jesus works *in* the believer, in order to his recovery. He breaks down the hard heart, arrests the soul in its onward progress of departure, places upon it some powerful check, lays it low, humbles, abases it, and then draws from it the blessed acknowledgment, " Behold, I am vile; but, he restoreth my soul."

There is infinite *wisdom*, too, in the Lord's restorings. This perfection of Jesus is clearly revealed here: in the *way* he adopts to restore, we see it. That he should make, as he frequently does, our very *afflictions* the means of restoration to our souls, unfolds the profound depth of his wisdom. This was David's prayer,—" Quicken me according to thy judgments ": and this was his testimony,—" Before I was afflicted I went astray, but now have I kept thy word ";—" Though I walk in the midst of trouble, thou wilt revive me." The season of trial is not unfrequently the sanctified season of revival. Who that has passed through the furnace has not found it so? *Then* the declension of the soul has been discovered,—*then* the hidden cause of that declension has been brought to light,—*then* the spirit has bowed in contrition before the Lord,—*then* grace has been stirred up in the heart, and a new sweetness has been given to prayer, and a new impulse to faith, and a new radiance to hope, and from the flame the gold and the silver have emerged, purified of their tin and dross. But for the production of effects like these, why the many peculiar and heavy afflictions that we sometimes see overtaking the child of God? Think not that our heavenly Father takes pleasure in chastening us; think not that it delights him to behold the writhings, the throes, and the anguish of a wounded spirit; think not that he loves to see our tears, and hear our sighs and our groans under the pressure of keen and crushing trial. No: he is a tender, loving father; so tender and so loving, that not one stroke, nor one cross, nor one trial more does he lay upon us, than is absolutely needful for our good;—not a single ingredient does he put in our bitter cup, that is not essential to the perfection of the remedy. It is for our profit that he chastens, not for his pleasure; and that often to rouse us from our spiritual sleep, to recover us from our deep declension, and to impart new vigour, healthiness, and growth, to his own life in the soul.

Nor must we overlook the *gentleness* of the Lord's restoring. We have a beautiful exhibition of this in the recovery of the stray sheep, as set forth by Jesus himself: "What man of you, having an hundred sheep, if he lose one of them, doth not leave the ninety and nine in the wilderness, and go after that which is lost, until he find it? And when he hath found it, he layeth it on his shoulders, rejoicing." Luke xv. 4, 5. Here is the gentleness of the shepherd,—" he layeth it on his shoulders." Too feeble itself to walk, too exhausted in its wanderings to return, the gentle shepherd having sought and found it, " lays it on his shoulders, rejoicing." Touching picture of the Saviour's gentleness in restoring a backsliding soul! What but infinite gentleness is seen in the restoring of Peter? It was but a *look*;—not a word fell from the lips of the Saviour—not an unkind rebuke, not a harsh upbraiding word did he breathe; yet *that* look—what artist's pencil has ever been able to imitate it;—that look so full of love, so full of gentleness, so full of forgiveness, did seem to say, " I am going to die for thee, Peter—all this and more I suffer for thee; wilt thou, canst thou deny me?"—that look, so touching, so melting, so eloquent, and so forgiving, reached the heart of the backsliding apostle, melted it, broke it, and sent him from the judgment-hall weeping bitterly. There was no expression in the look which Jesus bent upon Peter, but *love*. Let this truth be fixed in the heart of every backsliding believer. The Lord restores the soul *gently*. The moment he discovers to it its sin, he conveys some token of his pardoning mercy : the balm is applied the moment the wound is given, the remedy is at hand the moment the distemper is discovered. There is a tenderness, an unutterable tenderness, in the heart and hand, in the mercy and the method of the Lord's recovery of his child, which only he can feel. See it in the case of David. How did God bring his sin to remembrance? By the chastising rod? by heavy judgment? by severe expressions of displeasure? Nay; none of these were his messengers : but he sent a kind, tender, faithful prophet, to discover to him his awful backsliding; and the astounding words, " Thou art the man," had scarcely died away upon his ear, ere he pours in this healing balm, " The Lord also hath put away thy sin; thou shalt not die." Oh, what gentleness, what tenderness, are thus shown in the Lord's restorings of his wandering child! From whom could this have been expected but from him whose nature and whose name is *love*,—from whom, but him who could thus speak to his backsliding Ephraim : " Is Ephraim my dear son? is he a pleasant child? for since I spake against him I do earnestly remember him still; therefore my bowels are troubled for him : I will surely have mercy upon him, saith the Lord." This is an outgushing of tenderness towards a poor, returning, backsliding soul, which could only have had its dwelling-place in the heart of Jehovah.

But we have yet to speak of *the way* of a poor backslider's

return to the Lord. May the Spirit impart wisdom and unction in unfolding this most important point! First, as touching the *spirit* with which he should return.

Looking at the case of the backsliding church of Ephesus,
we find the nature of her sin, and the mode of her recovery,
thus set forth: "I have somewhat against thee, because thou
hast left thy first love. Remember, therefore, from whence
thou art fallen, and repent and do the first works." The first
exhortation addressed to her was, "Remember, therefore,
from whence thou art fallen." She was first called to solemn
reflection upon her former state of prosperity.

Let the backsliding believer be brought to this first step.
"*Remember* from whence thou art fallen";—revert to thy
past history, thy former spiritual state;—remember thy first
sorrow for sin, the first joy of its pardon;—remember the
spring-tide of thy first love—how precious Jesus was, how
glorious was his person, how sweet was his cross, how fragrant was his name, how rich was his grace;—remember how
dear to you was the throne of grace, how frequently you re-
sorted to it, regarding it of all spots on earth the most blessed;
—remember how, under the anointings of adopting love, you
walked with God as with a Father—how filial, how close,
how holy was your communion with him;—remember the
seasons of refreshing in the sanctuary, in the social meeting,
in the closet, how your soul did seem to dwell on the sunny
sides of glory, and you longed for the wings of a dove that you
might fly to your Lord:—remember how, publicly and before
many witnesses, you put off sin and put on Christ, and turning your back upon the world, took your place among the
followers of the Lamb;—remember how holy, and circum-
spect, and spotless was your walk, how tender was your conscience, how guileless was your spirit, how humble and lowly
your whole deportment. But *what* and *where* are you now?
O remember *from whence* you are fallen! Think from what
a high profession, from what an elevated walk, from what

holy employments, from what hallowed joys, from what sweet delights, and from what pleasant ways have you declined? May you not truly inquire with the sweet poet of Olney,—

" Where is the blessedness I knew
  When first I saw the Lord?
Where is the soul-refreshing view
  Of Jesus and his word?

" What peaceful hours I once enjoyed!
  How sweet their mem'ry still;
But they have left an aching void,
  The world can never fill.

" Return, O holy Dove, return,
  Sweet messenger of rest!
I hate the sins that made thee mourn,
  And drove thee from my breast."

In the exhortation given to the backsliding church at Ephesus, there is yet another instruction equally applicable to the case of all wanderers from the Lord: " Repent and do the first works." How can a departing soul return without *repentance*? by what other avenue can the prodigal reach his Father's heart? Repentance implies the existence and conviction of sin. Ah! is it no *sin*, beloved reader, to have turned thy back upon God? is it no *sin* to have lost thy first love, to have backslidden from Jesus, to have transferred thy affections from him to the world, or to the creature, or to thyself? is it no *sin* to go no more with the Shepherd, and to follow no more the footsteps of the flock, and to feed no more in the green pastures, or repose by the side of the still waters? O yes! it *is* a *sin* of peculiar magnitude; it is a sin against God in the character of a loving Father, against Jesus in the character of a tender Redeemer, against the Holy Spirit in the character of a faithful Indweller and a Sanctifier; it is a sin against the most precious experience of his grace, against

the most melting exhibitions of his love, and against the most
tender proofs of his covenant faithfulness.

Repent, then, of this thy sin.   Think how thou hast
wounded Jesus afresh, and *repent*; think how thou hast re-
quited thy father's love, and *repent*; think how thou hast
grieved the Spirit, and *repent*.   Humble thyself in dust and
ashes before the cross, and, through that cross, look up again
to thy forgiving God and Father.   The sweet promise is,
" They shall look upon him whom they have pierced, and
shall mourn for him as one mourneth for his only son."   This
leads us to touch upon one more point of vast moment in the
way of a soul's return to God.   It is this :

All real return of a backsliding soul is through Jesus.   Jesus
is God's great Door of approach to his throne.   No other entrance will conduct us to the golden sceptre; no other will
bring us into the holy of holies.   Thus has the Holy Ghost
unfolded this truth : " Having, therefore, brethren, boldness to
enter into the holiest by the blood of Jesus, by a new and
living way, which he hath consecrated for us through the
veil, that is to say, his flesh; and having an High Priest over
the house of God; let us draw near."   O blessed Door of return for a poor, backsliding, heart-broken believer !—a crucified Saviour, in whom God is well pleased, and for whose sake
he can receive the sinner, and put away his sin, can welcome
the backslider, and heal his backsliding.

Nor must we overlook the gracious *work of the Spirit* in the
restoring of a backsliding soul; but for him, not a step in the
way of return would be taken on the part of the believer.
The first solemn reflection, the first wistful glance of the eye
towards the Father's home, the first sigh that heaves the heart,
the first tear that starts from the fountain of grief, the first
step bent towards a forsaken God, is the effect of his blessed
operation, of his unchangeable love, and covenant faithfulness.   What debtors are we to the blessed and Eternal Spirit !
What reverential views should we entertain of his person, and

what tender thoughts should we cherish of his work!

The *encouragements* to return to the Lord are many and great: in the first place, we have *the gracious invitations of God himself.* How numerous and touching are these! Where is the heart, deeply conscious of its backsliding, that can resist the power of language like this: Go, and proclaim these words towards the north, and say, Return, thou backsliding Israel, saith the Lord; and I will not cause mine anger to fall upon you: for I am merciful, saith the Lord, and will not keep anger for ever." Jer. iii. 12. Here is a warrant for your return—God's own free invitation! You want no more. What if Satan discourages, what if your sins plead against you, what if guilt and unbelief and shame combine to impede your way, if God says, "Return!"—that is sufficient for thee. Thou dost want no more; if he is willing to receive you back, to pardon your sins, to forget your base ingratitude, to heal your backslidings, and restore your soul, you have the broad warrant to return, in the face of all opposition and discouragement. Yet again the cheering invitation runs,—"Only acknowledge thine iniquity that thou hast transgressed against the Lord thy God."—"Turn, O backsliding children, saith the Lord, for I am married unto you." "Return, ye backsliding children, and I will heal your backslidings." "I will heal their backsliding, I will love them freely: for mine anger is turned away from him." Jer. iii.; Hosea xiv.

The *character of God* is such as encourages the return of a backsliding soul. In the invitations he has given, he urges them upon the ground of *what he is*: "Return, thou backsliding Israel, saith the Lord; and I will not cause mine anger to fall upon you: *for I am merciful,* saith the Lord." O touching, soul-subduing, heart-melting argument,—"Return unto me, *for I am merciful!*" Merciful to receive you, merciful to pardon you, merciful to heal you. O the boundless mercy of God in Christ towards a soul returning from its wanderings! Will not this draw you? Again; "I have

blotted out as a thick cloud thy transgressions, and as a cloud
thy sins; return unto me, *for I have redeemed thee*." "Return, for I *have* blotted out thy transgressions: return, for I
have put away thy sins: return, for I *have* redeemed thee.
The work is already done,—the pardon has already gone
forth,—the backsliding has already been forgiven; then linger
not, but return, for I have redeemed thee." Here, on the
broad basis of the Lord's free and full pardon, the wandering
soul is urged to return. Truly may the apostle say, "If we
confess our sins, he is *faithful* and *just* to forgive us our sins,
and to cleanse us from all unrighteousness."

Thus is the character of God, as a merciful, sin-pardoning
God, held out in the word as a motive and an encouragement
to return. This is just the view of God, which, as a backsliding soul, you want. In yourself you see everything to
discourage, everything to forbid your return: and even on
awakening to a sense of your departure, your first thoughts of
God are such as to repel you from his presence; you are ready
to say, "I have wilfully departed from the Lord; I have gone
after other lovers; I have hewn out other cisterns; now the
Lord has given me up in his displeasure, and has forsaken me
for ever in his wrath." But God comes forth, and vindicates
his own gracious character, unfolds his own love, and in accents most encouraging and persuasive, addresses himself to
his wandering child, and says, "Return, thou backsliding
Israel, FOR *I am merciful*."

In the parable of the *prodigal son*, we have the character of
God towards a returning soul truly and beautifully drawn.
The single point we would now advert to is, the posture of the
father on the approach of his child. What was that posture?
—the most expressive of undiminished love, of yearning tenderness, of eagerness to welcome his return. Thus is it described: "And when he was a *great way off*, his father saw
him, and had compassion, and ran, and fell on his neck, and
kissed him." All this is God to thee, dear returning soul! He

is on the eager watch for thy first movement towards him; he is looking as with outstretched neck for the first sign of thy soul's return, for the first sound of thy footsteps, for the first relentings of thy heart: yea, even more than this, or this were nothing, he sends his own Spirit to work that return in thy soul, to break thy heart, to rouse thy slumbering spirit, to draw thee, win thee to his arms. This is thy God,—the God whom thou hast forsaken, from whose ways thou hast declined, but who, in the very depth of thy declension, and in the very extremity of thy departure, has never withdrawn his eye of love one moment from thee.

Nor must we overlook the grand source of encouragement to a returning soul,—*that which springs from the cross of Christ.* But for a crucified Saviour, there could be no possible return to God; in no other way could he consistently with the holiness and rectitude of the Divine government, with what he owes to himself as a just and holy God, receive a poor wandering, returning sinner. Mere repentance and humiliation for, and confession of, sin, could entitle the soul to no act of pardon. The obedience and death of the Lord Jesus laid the foundation, and opened the way for the exercise of this great and sovereign act of grace. The cross of Jesus displays the most awful exhibition of God's hatred of sin, and at the same time the most august manifestation of his readiness to pardon it. Pardon, full and free, is written out in every drop of blood that is seen, is proclaimed in every groan that is heard, and shines in the very prodigy of mercy that closes the solemn scene upon the cross. O blessed door of return, open and never shut, to the wanderer from God! how glorious, how free, how accessible! Hither the sinful, the vile, the guilty, the unworthy, the poor, the penniless, may come. Here, too, the weary spirit may bring its burthen, the broken spirit its sorrow, the guilty spirit its sin, the backsliding spirit its wandering. All are welcome here. The death of Jesus was the opening and the emptying of the full heart of God; it was the outgushing of that ocean of infinite mercy, that heaved and panted and longed for an outlet; it was God showing *how* he could love a poor, guilty sinner. What more could he have done than this? what stronger proof, what richer gift, what costlier boon, could he have given in attestation of that love? Now it is the *simple belief* of this, that brings the tide of joy down into the soul. It is faith's view of this that dissolves the adamant, rends asunder the flinty rock, smites down the pyramid of self-righteousness, lays the rebellious will in the dust, and enfolds the repenting, believing soul in the very arms of free, rich, and sovereign love. Here, too, the believer is led to trace the sin of his backsliding in its darkest lines, and to mourn over it with his bitterest tears,—

> "Then beneath the cross adoring,
>   Sin doth like itself appear;
> When the wounds of Christ exploring,
>   I can read my pardon there."

If the Lord has restored thy soul, dear reader, remember why he has done it,—*to make thee hate thy sins*. He hates them, and he will make thee to hate them too: and this he does by pardoning them, by sprinkling the atoning blood upon the conscience, and by restoring unto you the joys of his salvation. And never is sin so sincerely hated, never is it so deeply deplored, so bitterly mourned over, and so utterly forsaken, as when he speaks to the heart, and says, "Thy sins *are forgiven* thee, go in peace." As though he did say, "I have blotted out thy transgressions, I have healed thy backslidings, I have restored thy soul; 'that thou mayst remember and be confounded, and never open thy mouth any more because of thy shame, when I am pacified toward thee for all that thou hast done, saith the Lord God.'" Ezek. xvi. 63.

Remember that, *just where the departure commenced, there should commence the return*. Did it begin at the closet?— then at the closet let thy restoration commence. Return to

secret, closet prayer; build up the ruined altar,—rekindle the
expiring flame, let that holy sanctuary once more witness to
your confessions, your humiliations, your strong crying and
tears, and your close, filial, and hallowed communion with
God. O blessed moment that sees you there again, even
though it be to smite in anguish on your breast, and to cover
yourself with sackcloth and ashes before the Lord!

And do not overlook, in this great business of restoration,
*the intercession of Jesus, the High Priest, at the right hand of
God.* If thy heavenly Father has restored thy soul, not only
has he done it from the spring of his own unchangeable love,
but that which has prevailed with him was the power of the
sweet incense of the Redeemer's blood before the mercy-seat.
Moment by moment does this fragrant cloud go up, bearing as
it ascends all the circumstances of all the Israel of God. There
is not only the blood already sprinkled on the mercy-seat,
which has satisfied Divine justice, but there is the constant
pleading of the blood by Jesus, the Priest, before the throne.
O precious thought, O comforting, encouraging truth, for a
soul retreading its steps back to God! Of its own it hath
nothing to plead but its folly, its ingratitude, its wretchedness,
and its sin; but faith can lay its trembling hand upon this
blessed truth,—faith can descry Jesus clothed in his priestly
garments standing between the soul and God, spreading forth
his hands, and pleading on behalf of the returning believer the
merits of his own precious obedience and death. And thus
encouraged, he may draw nigh and touch the sceptre: "If
any man sin, we have an Advocate with the Father, Jesus
Christ the righteous." "Christ is not entered into the holy
places made with hands, which are the figures of the true; but
into heaven itself, *now* to appear in the presence of God for
us." Heb. ix. 24.

In view of all these precious encouragements, persuasive
motives, and earnest expostulations, will you, dear backsliding soul, still refuse to return? I entreat you, I implore you,

I beseech you, to arise and go to your Father, and say unto him, " Father, I have sinned against heaven and in thy sight." By all that is tender and forgiving in that Father's heart,— by all that is melting, persuasive, and precious in the work of Jesus,—by his agony and bloody sweat, by his cross and passion, by his death, burial, and resurrection, I beseech you to return! By the honour of that holy religion you have wounded, by all the hopes of glory you have indulged in, by all that is sacred and precious in the memory of the past, and by all that is solemn and real in the prospect of the future, I implore you to return! By the faithful promises of God, by the tender yearnings of Jesus, by the gentle drawings of the Spirit, by all that you will experience in the joy and peace and assurance of a restored soul, by the glory of God, by the honour of Christ, by the nearness of death and the solemnity of the judgment, I entreat, I implore, I beseech you, wanderer, prodigal, to return!

> " Return, O wanderer, return !
> And seek an injured Father's face;
> Those warm desires that in thee burn,
> Were kindled by reclaiming grace.

> " Return, O wanderer, return !
> Thy Saviour bids thy spirit live;
> Go to his bleeding side, and learn
> How *freely* Jesus can forgive.

> " Return, O wanderer, return !
> Regain thy lost, lamented rest;
> Jehovah's melting bowels yearn
> To clasp his Ephraim to his breast."

CHAPTER IX

THE LORD, THE KEEPER OF HIS PEOPLE

" The Lord is thy keeper."—Psalm cxxi. 5.

How frequently, clearly, and solemnly does the Holy Ghost unfold this great truth in his word, that salvation is entirely in and of God, irrespective of all worth, worthiness, or power of the creature; and that as the salvation of his covenant people is supremely and solely his own work, so in every respect it is infinitely worthy of himself. God can do nothing but what harmonises with his own illimitable greatness : he can never act below himself. All the productions of his creative power in nature, all the events of his directive wisdom in providence, bear the impress, from the smallest to the greatest, of his " eternal power and Godhead." But in salvation, it is supremely and pre-eminently so. Here, the whole Deity shines : here, the entire Godhead is seen; here, Jehovah emerges from the veiled pavilion of his greatness and glory, and by one stupendous exercise of power, and by one august act of grace, and by one ineffable display of love—before which all other revelations of his glory seem to fade away and well-nigh disappear—walks abroad among men in his full-orbed majesty : " And I heard a great voice out of heaven, saying, Behold, the tabernacle of God is with men, and he will dwell with them, and they shall be his people, and God himself shall be with them and be their God." This glorious " tabernacle " that is " with men," what less is it than the manifestation of Jesus in our own nature—God manifest in

the flesh? Truly may we say, "His glory is great in our salvation." Is he the only-wise God?—his salvation must needs
be the most profound result of that wisdom. Is he most holy?
—his salvation must be holy. Is he just?—his salvation must
be just. Is he gracious?—so must be his salvation. It bears
the imprint of every attribute; it embodies in its nature the
manifestation of every perfection. No other conception of
his wisdom, no other product of his power, no other revelation of his greatness, gives any adequate conception of God,
but the cross of his beloved Son. "It is here that he appears
under the new and unequalled aspect of the God of our salvation; and hence that he desires a renewal of praise, not only
for his excellent greatness, or his marvellous works, but for
what he is in his inherent and illimitable goodness, and for
what he imparts in the fruitions of his love. The very
thought of such a discovery, is itself a new creation. It is the
product of inspiration, not of mortal intelligence: it could
proceed only from him by whom it is to be substantiated and
accomplished; it constitutes its own evidence, it authenticates
itself. Divinity is not more its object than its essence: incom-
municable majesty is impressed on every feature, and diffused
over all its form. Well may it be said of such a system, even
as of Him who is its author, that herein God is manifested in
the flesh, beheld in his express image and his uncreated
brightness."

Now this salvation, thus so completely and entirely out of
the creature, in God, takes in all the circumstances of a child
of God. It is not only a salvation from wrath to come—that
were an immeasurable act of grace—but it is a *present* salvation, anticipating and providing for every exigency of the life
that now is, including deliverance from all evil, help in all
trouble, comfort in all sorrow, the supply of all want, and
through all conflicts, assaults, and difficulties, perfect safety
and final triumph. But the single point with which we now
have to do, is, the present and certain security of the believer,

provided for in the covenant of grace, made sure in Jesus the covenant head, and revealed in this glorious covenant plan of salvation. We have, in the preceding chapter, been considering the inherent tendency and the constant liability of a child of God to departure from God; we now would look up to the Holy Spirit to unfold to us this great and consoling truth, that in the midst of all their weakness, waywardness, and tendency to wander, the Lord is the keeper of his people, and that they whom he keeps are well and eternally kept. "The Lord is thy keeper."

We cannot rightly discuss our subject, without laying its foundation in the *perfect weakness of the believer himself.* If this were not so,—if there were aught of self-power in the believer, any ability to keep himself,—if he were not weakness, all weakness, and nothing but weakness,—then the Lord could not in truth be said to be the *keeper* of his people. This truth, we repeat, is the ground-work of our subject, and of it the believer needs to be perpetually put in remembrance. The principle of self-confidence is the natural product of the human heart: the great characteristic of our apostate race, is, a desire to live, and think, and act, independently of God. What is the great citadel, to the overthrow of which Divine grace first directs its power? what is the first step it takes in the subjection of the sinner to God? what, but the breaking down of this lofty, towering, independent conceit of himself, so natural to man, and so abhorrent to God? Now, let it be remembered, that Divine and sovereign grace undertakes not the extraction of the *root* of this depraved principle from the heart of its subjects. The root remains to the very close of life's pilgrimage: though in a measure weakened, subdued, mortified, still it remains; demanding the most rigid watchfulness, connected with ceaseless prayer, lest it should spring upward, to the destruction of his soul's prosperity, the grieving of the Spirit, and the dishonouring of God. O how much the tender, faithful discipline of a covenant God may have the subjection and mortification of this hateful principle for its blessed end, who can tell? We shall never fully know until we reach our Father's house, where the dark and, to us, mysterious dealings of that loving Father with us here below, shall unfold themselves in light and glory, elevating the soul in love and praise!

That no mere creature, angelic or human, can keep itself, is a truth fairly written out in the word of God, and illustrated by some of the most solemn and affecting examples. *In the history of the fallen angels*, God has revealed and confirmed this truth. If any creature could have kept itself from falling, why not a pure angelic spirit? All that the creature could possess in itself favourable to its security, they had; God created them in perfect uprightness and holiness; they were bound by a law implanted in their nature,—the same as the law of nature inscribed on Adam's heart, and which in substance corresponds with the moral law,—they were bound, we say, by this law to love God supremely, to obey him implicitly, to serve him devotedly and everlastingly. No power could release them from this obligation; nor did they want the moral capacity to obey it. The bent of their wills, the bias of their minds, the desire of their affections, were all towards it. And yet they fell! Why? Because God left them to the freedom of their wills, which were mutable; and that instant they were left to themselves, they fell as lightning from heaven. " I beheld," said Christ, " Satan as lightning fall from heaven." If it had been possible for created power to have sustained itself, here was the glorious theatre for the display of that power. Their natures were holy, the God whom they served was holy, the place they inhabited was holy, their companions were holy, their employments were holy, and yet they fell! Again we ask why?—because no creature ever has or ever can, by any innate, inherent strength or power of his own, keep himself; that moment God leaves him to himself, that moment he falls.

Look at Adam: he too was created in perfect holiness; not a taint of sin originally in his nature; not a cloud darkened his mind; not the least bias of his will, or a single inclination of his heart, but centred in God: and yet, he fell from his original holiness. And why? Because he could not keep himself: God left him to his natural and moral ability, which in the creature is natural and moral *weakness*, he left him to his own free-will, he left him to his own innate power, and the sad consequence was, he instantly fell, and in him, as their federal head, fell the whole human race. Adam was poor in himself,—he was a pensioner upon the free bounty of the God of heaven; even when he reposed amid the beauty and luxuriance of paradise, and trod the earth as the monarch of a new and a glorious world, every object of which paid him homage and submitted to his will, even then was he, as all creatures necessarily must be, poor in himself, and hung as a weak dependent creature upon the God that created him. And the moment that God withdrew his sustaining power, that moment Adam tore the crown of creature glory from his head, and trampled it into atoms in the dust!

Look at the histories of some of the most eminent of God's saints. What affecting confirmation do they afford to the most important truth we are now upon, that the creature left to itself is perfect weakness! If the angels in their purity, if Adam in his state of innocence, fell in consequence of being left in the sovereign will of God to their own keeping, what may we expect from a fallen, sinful, imperfect creature, even though renewed? Do we look into God's blessed word, and read what is there *declared*, touching the power of a renewed creature to keep itself? How affecting, and at the same time conclusive these declarations are: "Having no might"; "Without strength"; "Weak through the flesh"; "Out of weakness were made strong." Could language more forcibly set forth the utter weakness of a child of God? And what are the *figures* employed to impress upon the mind the same truth? They are most expressive; the believer is represented as a " lamb among wolves,"—as a dove ready to be fastened upon by the vulture,—as a " lily among thorns,"—as " a bruised reed,"—as " smoking flax,"—as a feeble branch hanging upon the vine. And what are their own *acknowledgments*? " The Lord is the strength of my life "; " The Lord is my shepherd "; " Hold thou me up, and I shall be safe "; " Keep back thy servant also from presumptuous sins "; " Hold up my goings in thy paths, that my footsteps slip not "; " We had the sentence of death in ourselves, that we should not trust in ourselves "; " Yet not I, but the grace of God which was with me "; " By the grace of God I am what I am." And what are the *examples*? To select but a few from among many: look at the intemperance of Noah, the unbelief of Abraham, the adultery and murder of David, the idolatry of Solomon, the self-righteousness of Job, the impatience of Moses, the self-confidence, and trimming, temporising policy of Peter. Solemn are these lessons of the creature's nothingness; affecting these examples of his perfect weakness!

But why speak of others? Let the reader, if he is a professing child of God, pause and survey the past of *his own life*. What marks of perfect weakness may he discover; what evidences of his own fickleness, folly, immature judgment, may he trace; what outbreakings of deep iniquity; what disclosures of hidden corruption; what startling symptoms of the most awful departure and apostasy from God, does the review present! And this, too, let it be remembered, is the history of a believer in Jesus, a renewed child of God, a partaker of the Divine nature, ar, expectant of eternal glory! Holy and blessed are they who, as they read and lay aside this book, shall relinquish all their fond conceit of self-power, and of self-keeping, and shall pray, and cease not to pray, " Lord, hold thou me up, and I shall be safe!" " Let him that thinketh he standeth, take heed lest he fall."

But the Lord will cause his people to *know* their perfect weakness and insufficiency to keep themselves, and that, too, not notionally, not theoretically, nor from what they hear, or from what they read, but from their own deep personal experience of the truth : yea, he is perpetually causing them to learn it. I do not allude merely to that blessed period when the Holy Ghost first lays his axe at the fabric of their self-righteousness,—truly they first learn it then,—but it is a truth they become growingly acquainted with; it is a lesson they are made daily to learn; and he becomes the most perfectly schooled in it, who watches most narrowly his own heart, is most observant of his own way, and deals most constantly and simply with the cross of Jesus. With regard to the way which the Lord adopts to bring them into the knowledge of it, it is various. Sometimes it is by bringing them into great straits and difficulties, hedging up their path with thorns, or paving it with flints. Sometimes it is in deep adversity after great prosperity, as in the case of Job, stripped of all, and laid in dust and ashes, in order to be brought to the conviction and the confession of deep and utter vileness. Sometimes it is in circumstances of absolute prosperity, when he gives the heart its desire, but sends leanness into the soul. O how does this teach a godly man his own utter nothingness! Sometimes it is by permitting the messenger of Satan to buffet,—sending and perpetuating some heavy, lingering, lacerating cross. Sometimes by the removal of some beloved prop on which we too fondly and securely leaned,—putting a worm at the root of our pleasant out-spreading gourd, drying up our refreshing spring, or leading us down deep into the valley of self-abasement and humiliation. But the great school in which we learn this painful, yet needed and wholesome lesson, is, in *the body of sin* which we daily bear about with us. It was here Paul learned his lesson, as the seventh chapter of his letter to the church at Rome shows, and for which epistle the saints of God will ever have reason to praise and adore the blessed and Eternal Spirit: "I know that in me (that is, in my flesh,) dwelleth no good thing: for to will is present with me; but how to perform that which is good I find not. For the good that I would I do not; but the evil which I would not, that I do. Now if I do that I would not, it is no more I that do it, but sin that dwelleth in me. O wretched man that I am! who shall deliver me from the body of this death?" In this school and in this way, did the great apostle of the Gentiles learn that the most holy, deeply taught, useful, privileged, and even inspired saint of God, was in himself nothing but the most perfect weakness of sin. Be not thou cast down, dear reader, if the Lord the Spirit is teaching you the *same lesson* in the *same way;* if he is now ploughing up the hidden evil, breaking up the fallow ground, discovering to you more of the evil principle of your heart, the iniquity of your fallen nature, and that, too, it may be, at a time of deep trial, of heavy, heart-breaking affliction. Ah! thou art ready to exclaim, "All these things are against me: 'I was at ease, but he hath broken me asunder; he hath also taken me by my neck, and shaken me to pieces, and set me up for his mark. His archers compass me round about; he cleaveth my reins asunder, and doth not spare; he poureth out my gall upon the ground. He breaketh me with breach upon breach, he runneth upon me like a giant.' Job xvi. 12-14. Am I a child of God? Can I be a subject of grace, and at the same time be the subject of so much hidden evil, and of such deep, overwhelming trial? Is this the way he dealeth with his people?"—

> " I asked the Lord that I might grow
> In faith, and love, and every grace,
> Might more of his salvation know,
> And seek more earnestly his face.

> " 'Twas he who taught me thus to pray,
> And he, I trust, has answered prayer;
> But it has been in such a way
> As almost drove me to despair.

" I hoped that in some favoured hour,
At once he'd answer my request,
And by his love's constraining power,
Subdue my sins, and give me rest.

" Instead of this, he made me feel
The hidden evils of my heart;
And let the angry powers of hell
Assault my soul in every part.

" Yea, more; with his own hand he seemed
Intent to aggravate my woe:
Crossed all the fair designs I schemed,
Blasted my gourds, and laid me low.

" ' Lord, why is this?' I trembling cried,
' Wilt thou pursue thy worm to death?'
' 'Tis in this way,' the Lord replied,
' I answer prayer for grace and faith.

" ' These inward trials I employ,
' From self and pride to set thee free,
' And break thy schemes of earthly joy,
' That thou mayst seek thy all in me.' "

Yes, dear believer, thou art not solitary nor alone: for along this path, all the covenant people of God are travelling to their better and brighter home. Here they become acquainted with their own weakness, their perpetual liability to fall; here they renounce their former thoughts of self-power and of self-keeping; and here, too, they learn more of Jesus as their strength, their all-sufficient keeper, more of him as their " wisdom, righteousness, sanctification, and redemption." Cheer up, then, for the Lord thy God is leading thee on by a safe and a right way to bring thee to a city of rest.

But, the Lord is the keeper of his people. To the consideration of this point, let us direct our remaining meditations. If what we have advanced touching the perfect helplessness, the proneness to constant departure of the child of God, be true, surely it needs no argument to show, that the believer stands in need of just such a keeper as God is. If he cannot keep himself, no mere creature can keep him—none but God in Christ.

Our blessed Lord has himself declared this truth. Mark the double security of the believer in his and his Father's hands: " My sheep hear my voice, and I know them, and they follow me : and I give unto them eternal life : and they shall never perish, neither shall any pluck them out of my hand. My Father, which gave them me, is greater than all; and none is able to pluck them out of my Father's hand. I and my Father are one." John x. 27-30. Here they are declared to be his own chosen peculiar people, his sheep; given to him of his Father, and perfectly safe in the hands of both. Listen to the breathing of his soul on behalf of his people: " And now I am no more in the world, but these are in the world, and I come to thee. Holy Father, keep through thine own name those whom thou hast given me, that they may be one as we are. While I was with them in the world, I kept them in thy name; those that thou gavest me I have kept."

That the Lord Jesus is *able to keep his people from falling*, is a view of our subject worthy of especial and grateful consideration. This is the ground-work of our faith,—that Christ has *power* to keep, through all time and to all eternity, the people entrusted to his care. They are his portion, his bride, his jewels; they were committed to him of his Father, and therefore he is responsible for their present and eternal salvation. Let us see how he is in all respects fitted for this great undertaking.

As God, Christ is able to keep his people. When Jehovah made promise of any blessing to his ancient people, with a view of confirming their faith in his ability to perform what he had promised, he was wont to append to his name Almighty, " *the Lord that created the heaven and the earth* " : so that, however great and stupendous, and seemingly impossible, might appear the thing primsed, He who "'created heaven and earth" was able to perform it. Now this very perfection of God, this work that stamps his omnipotence, and which answers all question and silences all doubts as to his "eternal power and Godhead," belongs and is ascribed *to Christ* the Keeper of his people. Thus,—"By him (Christ) were all things created that are in heaven and that are in earth, visible and invisible, whether they be thrones, or dominions, or principalities, or powers: all things were created by him and for him: and he is before all things, and by him all things consist." Col. i. 16, 17. Not less strikingly is the same exer-cise of omnipotent power applied to Christ in the epistle to the Hebrews,—"Who being the brightness of his [Father's] glory, and the express image of his person, *and upholding all things by the word o fhis power*, when he had by himself purged our sins, sat down on the right hand of the Majesty on high." Ch. i. 3. In this passage, Jesus is invested with a *crea-tive* and a *sustaining* power,—attributes that can be predi-cated only of God. Here lies, then, the great ability of Christ, as the Keeper of his covenant people. The same perfection which qualified him as the covenant head and surety of his people; the same almighty strength which enabled him to work out their salvation, to bear the burthen and the curse of their sins, enables him to preserve them while "dead in trespasses and in sins," and to keep them after they have been called and renewed by the operation of the Holy Ghost. As God, then, he is able to keep his saints from falling.

But, *as God-man Mediator*, he is also able to keep his people. As the covenant Head and preserver of his church, "it pleased the Father that in him should all fulness dwell." The Father knew what his beloved family would need. He knew what corruptions would threaten them, what tempta-tions would beguile them, what foes would assail them, what infirmities would encompass them, and what trials would de-press them; therefore it *pleased* him, it was his own good and gracious pleasure, that in his Son, the mediator of his beloved people, should *all* fulness dwell;—a fulness of merit, a fulness of pardon, a fulness of righteousness, a fulness of grace, wisdom, and strength, commensurate with the varied, multiplied, and diversified circumstances of his family. It is "*all* fulness." "Full," as Owen beautifully remarks, "to a sufficiency for every end of grace; full for practice, to be an example to men and angels as to obedience; full to a certainty of uninterrupted communion with God; full to a readiness of giving supply to others; full to suit him to all the occasions and necessities of the souls of men; full to a glory not unbecoming a subsistence in the person of the Son of God; full to a perfect victory in trials over all temptations; full to an exact correspondence to the whole law, every righteous and holy law of God; full to the utmost capacity of a limited, created, finite nature; full to the greatest beauty and glory of a living temple of God; full to the full pleasure and delight of the soul of his Father; full to an everlasting monument of the glory of God, in giving such inconceivable excellencies to the Son of man."

As the Mediator, then, of his people, he keeps them in perfect safety by night and by day. No man, no power, can pluck them out of his hands; he has undertaken their full salvation. To die for their sins, and to rise again for their justification, and yet not to provide for their *security* while travelling through a world of sin and temptation,—to leave them to their own guardianship, an unprotected prey to their own hearts' corruptions, the machinations of Satan, and the power of worldly entanglement,—would have been but a partial salvation of his people. Opposed by a threefold enemy,—Satan and the world in league with their own imperfectly renewed and sanctified hearts, that treacherous foe dwelling within the camp, ever ready to betray the soul into the hands of its enemies,—how could a poor, weak child of God bear up and breast this powerful phalanx? But he who was mighty to save, is mighty to keep; in him provision is made for all the trying, intricate, perilous circumstances in which the believer may be placed. Grace is laid up for the subjection of every inbred corruption,—an armour is provided for every assault of the foe,—wisdom, strength, consolation, sympathy, kindness,—all, all that a poor believing sinner can possibly require, is richly stored in Jesus, the covenant Head of all the fulness of God to his people.

But how is the child of God to avail himself of this provision? The simple but glorious *life of faith* exhibits itself here. It is by faith in Christ the soul is made strong in battle; this is the channel through which the fulness of Jesus comes to the believer. By faith he travels up to this rich and ample supply; by faith he takes his nothingness to Christ's all-sufficiency; by faith he takes his unworthiness to Christ's infinite merit; by faith he takes his weakness to Christ's strength, his folly to Christ's wisdom; his fearful heart, his timid spirit, his nervous frame, his doubtful mind, his beclouded evidences, his rebellious will, his painful cross, his peculiar case of whatever nature it may be, in the way of *believing*, in the exercise of *simple faith*, he goes with it to Jesus, and as an empty vessel hangs himself upon that "nail fastened in a sure place," the glorious Eliakim on whom is hung "all the glory of his Father's house, the offspring and the issue, all vessels of small quantity; from the vessels of cups, even to all the vessels of flagons." Isaiah xxii. 24. Thus may the weakest believer, the most severely assailed, the most deeply tried, the most painfully tempted, lay his Goliath dead at his feet, by a simple faith's-dealing with the fulness that is in Christ Jesus. O how mighty is the believer, who, in deep distrust of his own power, casting off from him all spirit of self-dependence, looks simply and fully at Jesus, and goes not forth to meet his enemy, only as he is "strong in the strength that is in Christ."

But what is the *great evil* of which the true saints of God most stand in jeopardy, and which their timid, fearful hearts most dread? Is it not *secret* and *outward backsliding* from God, after conversion? Surely it is, as the experience of every honest, upright, God-fearing man will testify. It is his consolation then to know, that Jesus is "able to keep him *from falling*"; "Unto him that is able to keep you from falling." Jude 24. This is the most overwhelming evil that stares the believer in the face. Some, but imperfectly taught in the word, are dreading awful apostasy from the faith here, and final condemnation from the presence of God hereafter,— believing that though Christ has made full satisfaction for their sins to Divine justice, has cancelled the mighty debt, has imputed to them his righteousness, has blotted out their iniquities, has called, renewed, sanctified, and taken full possession of them by his Spirit, and has ascended up on high, to plead their cause with the Father; that yet, after all this stupendous exercise of power, and this matchless display of free grace, they may be left to utter apostasy from God, and be finally and eternally lost. If there is one doctrine more awful in its nature, distressing in its consequences, and directly opposed to the glory of God and the honour of Christ, than another, methinks it is this.

Others, again, more clearly taught by the Spirit, are heard to say, "I believe in the stability of the covenant, in the unchangeableness of God's love, and in the faithfulness of my heavenly Father, but I fear lest some day, under some sharp temptation, some burst of indwelling sin, when the enemy shall come in as a flood, I shall fall, to the wounding of my peace, to the shame of my brethren, and to the dishonouring of Christ." Dear believer, truly thou wouldst fall, were he to leave thee to thine own keeping for one moment; but Jesus is able to keep thee from falling. Read the promises, believe them, rest upon them. Concerning his redeemed church, what does he say? "I, the Lord, do keep it; I will water it every moment, lest any hurt it; I will keep it night and day." Isa. xxvii. 3. "The Lord upholdeth the righteous." Psalm xxxvii. 17. "The righteous shall hold on his way, and he that hath clean hands shall be stronger and stronger." Job xvii. 9. "They go from strength to strength; every one of them in Zion appeareth before God." Psalm lxxxiv. 7. "They that trust in the Lord shall be as mount Zion, which cannot be removed, but abideth for ever. As the mountains are round about Jerusalem, so the Lord is round about his people, from henceforth, even for ever." Psalm cxxv. 1, 2. "Kept by the power of God, through faith, unto salvation." 1 Pet. i. 5. "I will lift up mine eyes unto the hills, from whence cometh my help. My help cometh from the Lord, which made heaven and earth. He will not suffer thy foot to be moved; he that keepeth thee will not slumber. Behold, he that keepeth Israel will neither slumber nor sleep. The Lord is thy keeper." Psalm cxxi. 1-5.

A simple glance at these passages will present to the believer's eye, a *threefold cord*, by which he is kept from falling. In the first place, *God the Father* keeps him,—"kept by the power of God"; the power that created and upholds the world, keeps the believer. The eternal purpose, love, and grace of the Father keeps him : this is the first cord.

Again, *God the Son* keeps him : "My sheep hear my voice, and I know them, and they follow me; and I give unto them eternal life; and they shall never perish, neither shall any man pluck them out of my hand." The covenant engagements, the perfect obedience, the atoning death of Immanuel, keeps the believer : this is the second cord.

Yet again, *God the Holy Ghost* keeps him : "When the enemy shall come in like a flood, the Spirit of the Lord shall lift up a standard against him" (marg. *shall put him to flight*). The effectual calling, the personal indwelling, the tender love, the covenant faithfulness, and the omnipotent power of the Eternal Spirit, keep the believer : this is the third cord. And "a threefold cord is not quickly broken." Eccles. iv. 12. Exceeding great and precious promises! Well may we sing with the poet—

> "More happy, but not more secure,
> The glorified spirits in heaven."

But with these promises of the triune God to keep his people from falling, he has wisely and graciously connected the diligent, prayerful use of all the means which he has appointed for this end. The believer is nowhere in the Bible spoken of, or addressed, as a lifeless machine, a mere automaton; but as one " alive unto God," Rom. vi. 11,—as " created in Christ Jesus," Eph. ii. 10,—as a " partaker of the Divine nature," 2 Pet. i. 4. As such he is commanded to " work out his own salvation with fear and trembling," Phil. ii. 12,—to " give diligence to make his calling and election sure," 2 Pet. i. 10,—to " watch and pray, lest he enter into temptation," Matt. xxvi. 41 : and the apostle Jude thus affectionately and earnestly exhorts the saints to whom he addressed his brief epistle, " But ye, beloved, *building up yourselves* on your most holy faith, praying in the Holy Ghost, *keep yourselves* in the love of God, looking for the mercy of our Lord Jesus Christ unto eternal life," 20, 21. Thus does God throw a measure of the responsibility of his own standing upon the believer himself, that he might not be slothful, unwatchful, and prayerless, but be ever sensible of his solemn obligations to " deny ungodliness and worldly lusts, and to live soberly, righteously, and godly, in this present world," remembering that he is " not his own, but is bought with a price."

Let the reader guard against the slightest abuse of any of the great truths discussed in this work, especially the one insisted upon in this chapter. If the power of God is the *efficient cause* of the eternal security of the believer, yet, as *auxiliaries* which God has appointed, and by which he instrumentally works, the believer is to use diligently all holy means of keeping himself from falling; as a temple of the Holy Ghost, as the subject of the Divine life, as a pardoned, justified man, he is called to labour perseveringly, to pray ceaselessly, and to watch vigilantly. He is not to run wilfully into temptation, to expose himself needlessly to the power of the enemy, to surround himself with unholy and hostile influences, and then take refuge in the truth, that the Lord will keep him from falling. God forbid! This were most awfully to abuse the "doctrine that is after godliness," to "hold the truth in unrighteousness"; and to make "Christ the minister of sin." Dear reader, watch and pray against this!

And lastly: Let the cheering prospect of that glory unto which you are kept, stimulate you to all diligent perseverance in holy duty, and constrain you to all patient endurance of suffering. In all your conflicts with indwelling sin, under the pressure of all outward trial, let this precious truth comfort you,—that your heavenly Father hath "begotten you again unto a lively hope, by the resurrection of Jesus Christ from the dead, to an inheritance incorruptible and undefiled, and that fadeth not away, reserved in heaven for you who are kept by the power of God through faith unto salvation"; that soon—O how soon!—all that now loads the heart with care, and wrings it with sorrow—all that dims the eye with tears, and renders the day anxious and the night sleepless, will be as though it had never been. Emerging from the entanglement, the dreariness, the solitude, the loneliness, and the temptations of the wilderness, you shall enter upon your everlasting rest, your unfading inheritance, where there is no sorrow, no declension, no sin; where there is no sunset, no twilight, no evening shades, no midnight darkness, but all is one perfect, cloudless, eternal day—for JESUS is the joy, the light, and the glory thereof.

"NOW UNTO HIM THAT IS ABLE TO KEEP YOU FROM FALLING, AND TO PRESENT YOU FAULTLESS BEFORE THE PRESENCE OF HIS GLORY WITH EXCEEDING JOY, TO THE ONLY WISE GOD OUR SAVIOUR, BE GLORY AND MAJESTY, DOMINION AND POWER, BOTH NOW AND EVER." *Amen.*